T0267840

2 TRANS 2 FURIOUS

An Extremely Serious Journal of Transgender Street Racing Studies

edited by
Tuck Woodstock
& Niko Stratis

ISBN: 979-8-218-23030-2

Cover illustration by Mattie Lubchansky
Edited by Niko Stratis & Tuck Woodstock
Zine design and painstaking layout by Shay Mirk & Niko Stratis

Published by Girl Dad Press
Printed by Radix Printing & Publishing Cooperative
2nd printing: July 2024

TABLE OF CONTENTS

Fast 10 Your Seatbelts: An Introduction
Tuck Woodstock

Not to set a speed record for alienating an entire readership, but I'm not a Fast & Furious fan per se. I've seen every film in the franchise exactly once[1] — and I use the word "seen" very intentionally, because I can't say that I've necessarily watched them. My meds-resistant-ADHD ass can only focus on an action scene for conservatively 45 seconds before finding myself getting up to grab a third beverage, or fiddling with the subtitles[2], or googling something like, "Can you drive from California to Brazil?"[3]

Granted, I'm a latecomer to the series, so I've never watched a Fast & Furious film as it's meant to be viewed: in a giant theater, speakers pounding, surrounded by whooping car guys. Instead, I screened them all with my roommates during the pandemic, lured in with promises that the protagonists would start by stealing VCRs and end by driving cars in outer space. Our movie marathon approach was neither fast nor furious; at one point, we paused *Fast & Furious 6* at the Car Salesman Humiliation Kink scene and forgot to finish the movie for six months.

---

[1] Except *Hobbs & Shaw*, which doesn't count because the title doesn't have a number in it so how am I supposed to remember where it goes? (Granted, *Tokyo Drift* doesn't have a number either, but that one is famously #3, except when it's #6. In conclusion, don't worry about it.)

[2] I can't say that I've really listened to these films, either, mostly due to Sound Mixing Crimes that force you to choose between missing 95% of the dialogue or being blasted by 150 db of VROOM VROOMs. We didn't have subtitles for *Fast & Furious 4*, and I still have no idea what happens in that one.

[3] Of course not!!! Imagine Brian and Mia trying to drive a sedan through the Darien Gap.

As such, you'd be right to ask whether I'm qualified to edit this zine,[4] or why I chose Fast & Furious as the focal point for my first book-shaped project. For the latter, my best explanation is that this franchise is a certified Rich Text, one that invites countless hours of analysis and debate.[5] There's hypermasculinity and homoeroticism and cop-killing and Cardi B. There's something called Race Wars; there's $15 million worth of free Corona ads.[6] The Rock performs a traditional haka with his daughter's youth soccer team. Gal Gadot appears, begging the question of whether BDS sanctions apply to individual actors, and dates a guy named Han Seoul-Oh. A car jumps between three skyscrapers in Abu Dhabi. We lose all grasp of how magnets work. Not since *CATS* (2019) has my desire to discuss a film with everyone I know been exactly equal to my desire to never watch that film again.

Outside of Fast & Furious, my go-to examples of Rich Texts all take place in alternate galaxies (*Lord of the Rings, Star Wars*) or more fanciful versions of our own world (*CATS, the Muppets, the Bible*). But I'd argue that Dom's crew lives in a world that's equally fantastic. As Roman observes in *F9*, the familia has become functionally invincible: enemies' bullets seldom hit their targets and horrific car crashes rarely cause even minor injury. Beloved characters return from the dead over and over again, their telenovela-style amnesia dissipated by the power of family. Even Paul Walker doesn't die — his CGI'd face smiles peacefully at Dom as he

---

[4] Again: Of course not!!! But I did edit the 2020 Portland visitors guide, which is in many ways the same. (Both contain references to streets.) I also have a degree in film production, which I completely forgot about until editing this essay.

[5] For example, I may have barely watched the movies, but I'm a devoted listener to The Worst Idea Of All Time podcast's sixth season, in which two New Zealand comedians watch the Fast & Furious films in reverse order and try to guess what's going on. They're watching the 9th movie nine times, then the 8th movie eight times, etc., so as I write this in May 2023, they're several months into the project and have barely made it to *Furious 7*. Patti Harrison stars in Episode 16 and I can't recommend it enough.

[6] Per a 2017 Insider article, so the figure is surely much higher by now.

drives away in what Vin Diesel calls "the best moment in cinematic history."[7]

As Niko and I put this zine together — both of us grappling with periods of grief and uncertainty in our day-to-day lives — we often remarked that working on this project was the bright spot in our weeks. Trans people don't exist in Fast & Furious World,[8] which means that nobody can hurt us there. I don't have to worry about our healthcare becoming criminalized in this fictional version of America, so I can focus on Charlize Theron's weird dreadlocks or Han's predilection for Kameda Kaki No Tane rice crackers. Do politicians want to exterminate us IRL? Sure, but we got Mattie Lubchansky to draw Dom morphing into a car, so who's winning here, really?

In all seriousness, I have been blown away by the creativity and originality of 2 Trans 2 Furious's contributors. The submissions we received included not only comics and collages, poetry and prose, but also a bingo card (pg. 88), a tabletop roleplaying game (pg. 45), a walking tour (pg. 39), and a Fast & Furious name generator (pg. 74). We even received several 3D sculptures and crafts, which we were tragically unable to include due to the nature of what a book is.

In 2 Trans 2 Furious, you'll find essays exploring the phenomena of demolition derby (pg. 49), car guys (pg. 13), and Cipher's bowl cut (pg. 63). Body horror queen Gretchen Felker-Martin sent us a story so viscerally upsetting that it took me multiple tries to read it all the way through (pg. 31) — a compliment, obviously — and Dizzy wrote the top-tier slashfic that we all deserve (pg. 67). Meanwhile,

---

[7] I need to give you the full quote because I think about it every day of my life: "It might be the best moment in cinematic history. Not just in my career but in cinematic history. Men around the world—everyone was able to cry—but men around the planet for the first time in history were able to cry together." MEN FOR THE FIRST TIME IN HISTORY WERE ABLE TO CRY TOGETHER!!!

[8] Johnny Tran exists, but that's different.

T.H. Ponders reimagines Fast & Furious in the style of *The Great Gatsby* (pg. 93), while Evan explains how every character represents a different Taylor Swift album (pg. 129). And of course, it wouldn't be a queer anthology without discussions of grief, objectification, homophobia, dysphoria, and Daddy dynamics.

Is this a frivolous use of our energy in These Trying Times? Perhaps, but this frivolous fantasy world we've created is one that trans people deserve to live in. It's been a joy to collaborate with nearly 50 trans people on a project that has absolutely zero stakes. In *2 Trans 2 Furious*, we are everywhere and we are in charge. We are hot and smart and fun and fast and furious. We're drinking Coronas at a BBQ on the rooftop; we're fucking in cars; we're breaking each other out of jail; we're choosing our families and our names. Nobody can kill us because we are invincible. Nobody can hurt us because if they try, we'll hit the NOS and speed away.

A Partial List of Suggestions We Received for the Title of This Zine
Contributor Collective

2 Trans 2 Drive
2 Trans 2 Gender
2 Fast 2 Trans
2 Fast But Never 2 Trans
Transitioning 2 Fastly

Rapid Onset Fender Euphoria
I Live My Life a Milligram at a Time
Fast and Furious: Transsexual Drift
I Like My Cars Fast and My Genders Trans'd
Every Car's Heart Is a Trans

Johnny Trans
RuDom's Drag Race
Charli XCX's VROOM VROOM
Putting the T in Toretto
Chosen Familia

You've Got a Fast Car, and I've Got a Plan to Tell You About My
"Mia Is Trans" Headcanon

Fast 4 Furious: Can't Host Will Travel
The Fast and the Fgender
Fast + Furious Fags
Trans & Genderous
The Fast & the Gender
The Trashed and the Glorious
The Queer and the Furious
Fast, Furious, and Trans as Hell
Stay Fast, Stay Trans
Fast Trans
TransFurious

Manual Transmission
Fast Trans Missions
Mass Transit
Fast MX
69 MPH
The Street Always Wins
Cars Don't Fly

Consistent & Persistent: Irreversible Damage We Received From
Watching Fast and Furious (Without Providing Informed Consent)

67,292 Things Car Guys Can Teach Transsexuals
Adrian Glenn

Sometimes when I think about being trans too much, I wonder if I have perhaps *too much* of a sense of self. I'm like, should I be thinking so much about who I am, instead of just being it? I crave relief from being *sort of like a kind of person* instead of just a person. I literally will eat cereal and think, "Right now, I am like one of those guys who eats cereal." But then I remember about car guys and I am like, well, they get it.

Car guys have a relationship to identity, aesthetic, performed masculinity, and deep special interest that is usually reserved for the neurodiverse transmasculine.

I think car guys are scared to die. They have found something they love so much, they have a clear idea of who they are, and they have plans. They are going to tint; they are going to sell and acquire Camaros; they are going to attend a car show at a beach town this October. They have full lives and, more than anything, they have each other. The queer community should pay close attention to the kinship patterns of car guys. I haven't read a whole lot about the bonds between car guys, but I did witness firsthand the way that the death of Paul Walker tore the community wide open. They grieved openly and together.

I have a dear friend who fell face-first in love with a committed, documented Car Guy. She seemed acutely aware that she would always come second for him, and I think she made her peace with that early on. She knew she would probably never love anything the way he loved cars. But I noticed how hard she tried to love him in exactly that way. She wanted to fix him up. She felt pride when she cleaned him, trimmed his beard. She had long-term goals for him. She picked out new outfits for him at Kohl's and bragged to him about her savings, as he interrupted with news about the fresh coat of paint that was going on his Honda Civic. She hoped he wouldn't get any on his shirt.

I remember the first time I saw *Tokyo Drift*. I was in the Middle of Nowhere, Pennsylvania. I was 15 and it was my first time at a new friend's house. She was beautiful and I wanted us to be touching with at least three additional limbs, but she had a boyfriend.

Thirty minutes into my visit, I suddenly just didn't want to be there anymore. I didn't feel angry, not really very sad at all either. I just longed to be elsewhere. A different place, with different people, within a different moment. And then every cell in my body pleaded to not feel that way in all of my moments, in every group of people, in all places. I learned early on that there is no shortage of people who live in cycles of continuous longing for what isn't present. They become unable to navigate the obstacles that stand between themselves and fulfillment, locked in stagnant misery.

Watching *2 Fast 2 Furious*, in this moment, I am mostly comfortable; I am not in immediate danger; I am loved and I love back; and I understand the future, not as a way out of this moment, or as a road of potential miseries laid bare before me, but as time—the time that I have left to, in many moments, feel mostly comfortable, not in immediate danger, and to love and be loved back. If this present moment is enough for a car guy, it's enough for me too.

This part is important: The runtime of *Tokyo Drift* is one hour and 44 minutes. If you adjust for work, commutes, sleep, and dentist appointments and consider that the average American gets 27,000 days to spend on this warming rock, we are left with 4,860 days worth of time to spend consciously. Friends, brothers, car guy allies, I report with manic delight that this is enough time to watch *Tokyo Drift* 67,292 times. Rounded down, no less!

I am trying hard not to say anything like "2001 action movies make me long for a boyhood I never had." I could have watched *The Fast and the Furious* in 2001 — I just didn't think it seemed very interesting. The Fast & Furious movies do, however, make me long to be a car guy. To have a non-politicized but very passionate and specific identity. To feel deeply for a thing that can never love me back. To have a tangible external manifestation of my sense of self. To laugh in the face of anyone who insinuates that an expensive lift kit or speed modification is frivolous. To implicitly respond, fuck you, I like it, and that's why I should have it! That is precisely how I feel about testosterone cypionate and I wish that was all we had to say on the issue.

Look, cars are wretched, and if they would just melt all cars down into a large cube and hurl it into the sky like a Katamari-inspired tombstone to the auto industry, I would buy a telescope to gaze at it with pride. I actually think that everyone except for car guys should move near cities and use public transport. A few times a year, we can pay a visit to car guys and tour their rural and suburban auto-centric kingdoms. We can take pictures of ourselves filling their cars with gas. I'll bring a sock full of quarters so that we can put air in their tires for them. It'll be like when I used to visit the Amish and work on the farm for a few hours as a kid.

In an interview about the loss of Paul Walker, co-star Jordana Brewster said that her grief "goes in waves where it's super visceral at times, and it's like it's unimaginable that that person's not with us anymore. It just gets very intense and then sometimes it's less intense."

I read that and said aloud, "Dude, you're so right." Grief isn't a several-stage process that you move through and then set aside. You just have to clench up and hope that you are lucky enough to access a hypothetical sweet spot in which the memories are there and clear, but they don't feel like being punched in the gut. That you can smile to yourself and say, "What a guy."

Car guys are so good at saying "what a guy." The Fast and the Furious is a series about saying "what a guy."

Adrienne Rich has a poem that I think describes grief well, but I think this part more accurately describes how it feels to watch the opening scene of *Tokyo Drift* on my crush's navy corduroy couch:

*"it will not be simple, it will not be long
it will take little time, it will take all your thought
it will take all your heart, it will take all your breath
it will be short, it will not be simple"*

A Poem Written by the Stretch of the US/Mexico Border That the Team Drives Under in a Tunnel at the End of the Fourth Movie of the Fast and the Furious Franchise, Which Is, Confusingly, Called *Fast and Furious* (The Movie Is Called That, Not the Stretch of the US/Mexico Border)

Lee Sessions

So the thing is, it was really nice before.

It was so quiet? And dark?

I mean, you should have seen the stars, it was crazy.

Actually, what I think I liked most was stretching into the hot sand.

I liked the heft of it. It was really, like, solid. Like more solid than solid.

I liked being alone.

I mean, I know that's a thing people say when they don't really like being alone but for me it was true.

I would just stretch into the hot sand and feel the solidity at the heart of me and look up at the endless stars and just, like, exist, you know?

I even liked the fence, the wall, whatever it was up there.

It made me feel important, kind of? Like, more present? Like people talked about me a lot but never exactly about ME, if you know what I mean.

I mean, of course sometimes I could feel something inside of me.
A sneaking or, like, a skittering.
I just kind of figured everyone feels that sometimes, like really
deep down, right? It's just that no one really talks about it, you
know.
That's what I figured.
And THEN, one night, I mean, it was the craziest thing.
There was so much NOISE inside of me?
Engines and yelling and revving and crashing and shit, I mean, I
don't really know much about cars but SOMETHING was
happening down there, really deep inside, and it was so MUCH
and it was so LOUD.
Honestly, I don't know, I don't really know how to describe it. It
was so crazy.
And then it ended, like, just as suddenly as it had begun?
And I was alone again and quiet again.
But I could still feel that hollow in the deepest part of me echoing,
like, in a way that meant it would keep echoing.
Like maybe forever?
And I could just feel myself being like, what the FUCK?
Honestly, like, what the ACTUAL fuck.
And what the FUCK am I supposed to do with all this HOT SAND
and all of these STARS now?

Letty Did Not Trans Me (But Maybe She Did!)
Mckenzee Griffler

Back when I was much less able to just let myself "be someone who was allowed to enjoy things," I had no connection to the Fast franchise, other than a generalized disinterest in the premise— despite being a longtime adherent of high concept, the-DVD-cover-explains-it-all cinema. It was around 2015, and I was a walking film degree living in NYC and having an existentially bad time, as you do when you know you have a major gender thing going on and you haven't yet worked up the courage to say you have a major gender thing going on. I was still in the bargaining stage: you know, the one where you compensate for suppressing the most obvious, basic fact about yourself by being the most compliant, boring person in Hoboken who would disappear into a wall if she stood still so nobody can say you're doing anything wrong and therefore you're safe and ok and you try not to consider the currents of the Hudson River for too long.

To paint another picture, the majority of my life at the time, if not editing video or standing around on a commercial film set, was spent walking the six blocks from my apartment to the Planet Fitness, listening to the entire Night Vale back catalog, and staring vacantly through the gym mirrors as I made my body different (the wrong kind of different than I actually needed, but y'know).

Anyways, my friend C, who I had gone to college with in California, was now living in Connecticut, and he *loved* the Fast & Furious movies. At least, I thought he must've loved them because he had them all on Blu-ray—but he also had, like, literally 200 other Blu-rays. So in retrospect, maybe I wouldn't rush to call him a real Fasthead, either.

I would occasionally take the bus to the subway to the Metro North to go visit him on weekends; to witness a different suburbia than the one I had tried to escape by moving to California and then New York; to have an attempted normal time outside of my eternally looping routine; to listen to him complain about my vegetarianism as he made meatballs for himself from his precise recipe he kept laminated; to hear his parents complain about everything and each other in a way that made me somewhat uncomfortable; to walk through Westport together in the summer, a place that had mansions but no sidewalks; and to watch a lot of movies together.

I can't really tell you whether we were friends in the platonically intimate sense, but he was familiar and didn't make me think too critically about much in the world, especially myself, especially as he never seemed too interested to ask me about me—not that I would've had much insight to share at the time beyond "please do not think too deeply about how I am." There was, however, something about the faintest traces of his vulnerability, the occasional surprising warmth among his deluge of complaints, and maybe even his hospitable nature. The way he carefully made my couch bed for me, tucking the corners just so, a gentle current underneath his straight boy posturing and grating snootiness. It was all somewhat compelling to me. I felt like I was maybe bearing witness to something that he was hesitant to share with anyone else in his life. It was reassuring, somehow. My bar for boys was pretty low at the time.

I came up for a three-day weekend; he picked me up from the train, and I remember how theatrically appalled he was that I had not seen the Fast and the Furious franchise (I think a new trailer might've just come out, spurring this revelation). And so, he decided on the spot that we were going to watch all seven films released up until that point in one sitting. I was in no position to have opinions in 2015, especially with the dissociative treat of seven movies in a row dangling in front of me.

So we watched (what I just googled and calculated to be) 958 minutes of cars going really fast, nobody orders the tuna sandwich, granny shifting not double clutching like you should, he moans like a cop, too many crucifix glamor shots, the exquisite brilliance of *Tokyo Drift* (the absolute best one, I will die on this hill), and that time that Vin Diesel could recreate a car crash in his mind to figure out what happened to Letty.

God, what a dumb franchise. I was instantly smitten.

For years afterwards, Fast was embedded as a constellation of stupid reference points in my brain. Come on, Bow Wow plays a character named *Twink* for god's sake. Did I later discover just how much the first one was basically a somewhat lazy reimagining of *Point Break*? Sure. Did I cry when they did that tribute to Paul Walker? No, because I wasn't on estrogen yet. But there was pathos there for sure.

There's probably a motivational TDOV speech where this ends with me having a moment of self-awareness as I watch Letty rediscover her identity somewhere around minute 500 of this marathon, causing my girl brain to rev to life, ending in a triumphant race to Callen-Lorde. Unfortunately, I wasn't suffering from car accident amnesia-inflicted supervillainy; I was just traumatized and didn't think I deserved nice things. So, I remained a boy* who liked the car movies and made others watch them too, to mixed results. Sometimes my pals would get absorbed by the fifth film, the kenshō that happens when you simply let your brain fall out and watch them swing a big safe around in Brazil with Dodge Chargers, somehow. Sometimes they would be wrong and not like the movies. Which is fine.

Anyways, a year later, I came out as trans (tepidly; apologetically; I got better at it eventually). Two years after that, C was living in Los Angeles as he had always hoped; I was there on a brief trip, and we had plans to get together for dinner. All I knew was that he was, let's say, *not the best* about accepting I wasn't a boy. I had never spoken with him about it directly— this was secondhand knowledge from another friend—but I was still learning about the concept of mattering, so I didn't push the issue of basic respect at the time.

We ended up not getting together due to a pretty boring scheduling conflict, which is what happens with LA traffic when you aren't in a cinematic universe with completely empty surface streets for racing on. Apparently, he was so upset about not being able to meet that he decided to never talk to me again, which is where that still stands, six years later. So, the weekend when we binged the entire franchise was the last time we ever hung out, after years of friendship and creative collaboration.

Whenever a new Fast movie comes out, I think about texting him, but really, it was always pretty superficial between us in the first place.

C, if you're reading this, I hope you agree that *Hobbs & Shaw* was a terrible movie.

My Daddy, the Rock:
A Transfeminine Haiku
Skylar Pape

I came fast—too fast.
How naughty! Daddy's not pleased.
Oh, he's furious.

Which one's fast and which one's furious?

A comic by AA and AK

AK breaks down the entire Fast and the Furious saga ...from memory.

Don't worry about spoilers, this comic is incoherent.

Okay, so the only thing I reeeally remember about the first one is the beginning where they're yelling about sandwiches in little mesh tank tops.

Ahh! You call that a sandwich?!

Paul Walker, a.k.a. Brian, is sitting at a cafe he frequents, flirting with Jordana Brewster, a.k.a. Mia, and orders a:

Tuna on white, no crust.

You can get a cheese and fries for 2.95 FAGGOT!

Hell of a deal, honestly.

I like the tuna.

24

Definitely thought we were gonna start with some sick car action, but. Tuna sandwich, mesh tank tops, out of this world combo meal prices, okay. I'm with it.

Oh, yeah. Well that too, but really it's all about family. And it's gay. You know?

2 Fast introduces Devon Aoki, who plays Suki in the film, important, and our good friend, Ludacris! The soundtrack is very Luda heavy.

Damn, Suki! When you gonna pop MY clutch?!

Also, Devon Aoki wears verrry small clothes and drives a pink car.

Soon as you get the right set of tools.

GAY!

I know!

I love that you've seen this one the most, but were NOT queer at the time...

Well, I didn't see D.E.B.S. until later, in D.E.B.S. Devon Aoki is smoking a cigarette and holding a gun!

Focus! This is about Fast and the Furious!

Right, right. I know. Okay, moving on....

The next one is unfortunately...

Yesssss! My personal favorite!

TOKYODRIFT!

Gus, you can't just decide the worst one is your favorite to annoy me. I'm not easily annoyed.

But Tokyo Drift does introduce us to Han! So fine!

Ahem! And Lil Bow Wow.

It's actually just Bow Wow now.

But yes, Tokyo Drift has Han, important. And Bow Wow, less important. And some random white guy that isn't any of the other white guys in the other movies, not imporant.

We are so fast, bro.

And furious, bro.

4-6 I don't really remember well because it's mostly just about cars.

Cars and family.

7 is a big one though, because that's the one where Paul Walker RUNS up a TRUCK falling off a CLIFF!

Wait, maybe a bus?

A truck or a bus. Whatever.

It's for sure a bus. But to be fair, it actually just looks like a tank.

Isn't that one famous because he literally died?

Well. Not in the movie. In the movie, he just becomes a stay at home dad.

Ok, ok. F8 What is happening here, is that a SUBMARINE?!

Who could really say?

I'm gonna be honest, I don't remember a lot, but I do remember there's a baby in it just vibing wearing headphones and someone yells:

I'm gonna kill! that! baby!

Definitely gonna watch that one.

Great! Can't wait to find out why they were gonna kill that baby.

Which brings us to 9! Where Charlize Theron does race science in a box!

A completely normal thing that I was definitely expecting.

I saw F9 in theaters. The first film I'd seen since COVID, and I don't remember a thing about it other than screaming the whole time. I don't know if there even is a plot.

AHHH HHH!!!

28

29

Enemies 2 Lovers
Al Larned

Family Vehicle
Gretchen Felker-Martin

My name is Dominic Toretto, and family is everything to me.

It has been six years since my team dragged what remained of my body from the fiery wreckage of my Charger, and four since my fusion with its shattered chassis and our strange shared rebirth. My father always said I had gasoline in my veins; he didn't know how right he was. I can feel it now, ebbing and surging to the beat of my heart through my fuel injectors and the dormant scar tissue of my combustion chamber. Staying clean. Staying ready. When gasoline stops circulating, the particulates in it can settle and form buildup. I never settle. I'm always on the edge. I can do zero to sixty in two point three without even breaking a sweat.

When I do sweat, my sister Mia has to open up my chassis and sponge what's left of my human parts down with disinfectant and antifungals, or else the points where I'm connected to the Charger turn necrotic. I protect my family, they protect me. When I have to get a tuneup it's Brian and Mia who come with me to the surgeon Han found for me on the Dark Web, one who knows enough about cars to work on all of me at once. When I need a shakedown it's Brian in my driver's seat. I can feel him in the strips of skin grafted onto the worn leather upholstery. I can feel his ass clench on tight turns and when his breathing slows as we come into a straightaway.

I can feel the tension in his thighs as he downshifts. Sometimes I can almost hear the thoughts roaring up and down his spine in an electrochemical torrent. It's been like that, since the accident. People get angry and I feel it in the air like static before a lightning strike. They keep a secret and I feel it like a weight on my shoulders.

I'm different now. Stronger, but more vulnerable, too. I need my family more than ever, but they're restless, itching to have their own lives, become their own people.

This is the story of how they came back to me.

We're on an assignment from Hobbs when it happens, hunting down a man named Owen Shaw. London. Narrow streets and nervous drivers. He surprises us when we think we have him cornered. His team's getaway cars, armored and low to the ground. Ramps with wheels. One of them swerves at just the right moment and as I scream in pursuit under a decrepit overpass my dash cam picks up Mia's Integra rolling through the air above us. I brake, or Brian does. Our nerves burn in tandem. My scream of loss and rage is tinny and garbled through the speakers, a wash of irate static, and we fishtail and slew and come around, narrowly missing a pair of drunk football fans. One throws an empty bottle. I can feel it shatter against my rear headlight, cracking the fiberglass housing. The Integra hits the street, flips twice, and bursts into flames as Shaw's man streaks away into this thicket of a city. Brian is already out and running.

He kicks in the Integra's window and drags her out. They're so close when the gas tank goes that it knocks him on his ass, but he gets up, shakes himself like a dog and keeps pulling her back toward me. Sirens blare in the distance, getting closer. Brian heaves her into the passenger seat. She's limp as a broken doll, skull fractured, skin sheared from most of her right side. Her head lolls on her shoulder as he reaches across her to fasten her seatbelt, blood spurting from her split scalp, and it's obvious her neck is broken. I can taste the salt and iron of her soaking into my hybrid upholstery. Her heartbeat flutters faint against me. My own jackhammers, the engine roaring in sympathetic desperation.

There's gasoline in Toretto blood.

"We have to get her to a hospital," he pants, coughing and red-faced. The Integra burns, the heat of it beating against us from twenty yards away.

I deactivate the dash clock. *No time.* I can see he understands.

"Dom... what can we do?"

My only answer is to slam my doors and pop the locks. He hammers on the window, shouting. I ignore him. Mia has minutes left, maybe less, and I have work to do. I concentrate on her seatbelt, on the nerves woven through the nylon, just beginning to reconnect to the grafts in the seat. It twitches. Mia's mouth falls open. She drools dark blood. I can feel her thoughts like flying shrapnel. *Dom* and *Brian* and *fire* and *leg* and *baby,* little particles of awareness borne on a wave of cognitive overload. Baby? Little tadpole squirming in her belly. No time for that. I will the belt to move. I gentle the engine, matching its rumbling rhythm to her heart's fading beat.

I'm here. I've got you, kid.

The bolt pops from the belt clip, displaced by a little ring of muscle growing like a barnacle inside the mount, and the strip of tough nylon sags, shivers, and begins to move. I feel like I'm operating a miniature crane game with my tongue. So clumsy. No time. God *damn it.* Brian is screaming. I pop the passenger door without warning, knocking him over, and he goes quiet. Lies still. Need to focus. The belt squirms across Mia's chest and up over her shoulder to curl around her neck. I pull it tight. The stump of my right arm is throbbing red-hot where it's bolted to the front right wheel well.

I can feel every inch of her where it touches me. In the infrared dome camera I can see the heat starting to fade from her limbs as her heart slows. I flex, feebly at first, then with a strength borne of desperation, and the seat's upholstery begins to tear. Her blood saturates the seatbelt. It pools around her shoes and soaks into the floor mat under them. Slowly, so slowly, sheets of upholstery tear loose and wrap themselves around her broken body. I taste her blood, her raw skin, the grit and broken glass ground into her. She shivers. The little finger of her left hand twitches.

I can feel it's going to work in the moment before it happens, like when you're about to come. That heat building inside you. Your thighs trembling. Your back bending like a bow. I scream into the oil and artificial amniotic fluid that circulate within my protective caul. New nerves, raw as stab wounds, push from my carself into Mia, finding hers where her injuries have left them exposed, wrapping themselves around that fragile network. The cascade of knowing and feeling is almost too much. I'll go crazy. Die. My hearts are beating. I am watching myself watching myself watching myself playing in the yard the kitchen father yelling Jakob broke the lamp the wrench the race the car the fire the first time first time first time fingers in my cunt I have a cunt his fingers are inside it and I'm crying, crying 'cause it feels so good and then the roll the Brian tuna sandwich Rio—

She draws a deep, shuddering breath. We draw it. We blink her eyes, one of which still works, and reach up with unfeeling fingers to pluck the sliver of glass from the other one. Upholstery knits itself around her injuries like a cocoon. That's when I notice Brian. He isn't moving. There's a dent in his skull where it struck the curb after I knocked him down, and it's swelling nastily. Mia panics, making wet sounds with her ruined mouth. Our heartbeats flutter again. I am trying to move tubing through the air conditioning vents, to work her into the same circulatory system, but it will take time.

Calm down, I tell her. We tell ourself. Disorienting to see through so many eyes at once, mechanical clarity and blurry organic depth. *I know how to do this.*

A minute's work and I extrude a floppy tentacle of seatbelts bound together with my grafted skin, guide it painstakingly across the street like a nylon snake slithering in slow motion, and wrap it tight around his ankle. I start to drag him toward the driver's side. We drag him. It's easier now that we're together. It'll be easier still once Brian's with us. A real family again. The sirens fade. The others must have drawn them off. No people here this late at night. A light rain falls as Mia's ears detect a motorcycle on approach.

Han screeches to a halt a few yards away, putting his boot down to slow his motorbike. "Dom," he says quietly. "What happened?"

"An accident," says Mia. I say it through her, but the words are hers. Ours.

An accident, mouths Brian, not waking.

"Are they okay?" he asks. He knows something is wrong. At least, that's how he sees it. I can smell his fear, hear his heartbeat in the air. I yank Brian up into the driver's seat and slam the door. It's so much more natural to open the upholstery for him. At once I feel the tingling in his fingers, see the migraine auras around Han and Mia. I catch ourselves in a loop when their eyes meet meet meet meat meat meet, and I feel an enormous satisfaction that they are no longer more important to each other than I am to them. The meat has met. I look away from myself. The tubing is wriggling out of the vents now. Seeking flesh. There is a powerful smell of gasoline and lubricant. I can feel Brian's father's hand on the back of my neck, callused and hard, and smell the Miller High Life on his breath. I can see Roman laughing.

"Are they okay?" Han asks again. Sweat beads at his temples.

"We're fine," says Mia, attempting a smile. A few teeth ooze out of her mouth to plop in the blood pooling in her lap. Baby. The baby.

"Fine," Brian husks. His hand finds the clutch. His foot drags leaden toward the brake pedal, but it is getting quicker. Stronger. Nothing is as strong as family. Did I say that out loud? With which mouth? It doesn't matter. Han is running, kick-starting his motorcycle and hauling it around, the little engine screaming, Han screaming, hurtling away into the rainy London night.

The Charger is faster.

We perform our own maintenance now. It is six months since the crash in London and I am in a derelict garage consuming what is left of Owen Shaw. There's a verse from Isaiah my grandma liked to quote when we were raising hell. *No weapon formed against me shall prosper.* The man who tried to kill my sister is our family now. No one has ever been as close as we are, bound vein to vein and lungs to gaskets, our nerves a crackling network interwoven through the Charger's Detroit steel. The trunk is where I keep the brains, bathing in a nutrient soup of synthetic blood and electrolytes. There isn't room for whole bodies anymore. I'm starting to forget what a body is. My thoughts disagree with themselves sometimes. I have to think them again and again, watching the words spiral out through loops of recursive consciousness until we find consensus. Until we're family again.

Shaw crawls away from me as I pluck shrapnel from myself. His spine is broken, his legs twisted. He leaves a smeared trail of black-red blood behind him, like a dying snail. He and his team put up a hell of a fight. Concealed explosives, armor-piercing ammunition, a high-speed chase with a tank concealed inside a long-haul truck. He tried to break my nerve, put Letty in danger. Until last year I didn't even know she was alive. Dreamed every night of her spreading herself hot and sticky to take the knob of my shifter inside her. Her breasts crushed against the dashboard, imprinted with the pattern of the AC vents. *I miss you, Dom. God, I miss you.*

She doesn't miss me anymore. She's in the caul with me now, our ruined bodies twined together, sheared and lumpy features sucking at each other, scars fusing to scars fusing to wounds fusing to steel. I had to open myself all the way to let her in. The Charger gapes, roof split, scarred and carbon-scored sides shivering as I vent hydraulic fluid. A dozen pairs of nimble hands sort through the mingled organs and components under my hood as I slowly advance in Shaw's wake. Some of me is screaming, still. It takes time to adjust to myself. Flesh tents parts of the Charger's fuselage, growing tight against her paint job. An eye blinks just under the right-hand side mirror. Ears quiver along the sides of her nose. When we speak it is my voice, my dark velvet purr, which emerges from the mouth of flesh and metal hidden just behind her grille.

"Come on, Shaw. Your team's dead. Your job's over. You wanna die alone?"

"Fucking monster," he growls, commando-dragging himself another pitiful few inches with his one good arm. All around us are his fellow mercenaries, splattered and burst like roadkill, smashed into jelly against the garage's walls. I pluck a shard of one of their skulls from my windshield and flick it away to clatter on the concrete floor. We creep a little closer. My minds direct a quartet of swaying, many-jointed arms out through my open windows, plucking at Shaw's boots, his trousers, his bloody shirt and jacket. I am Gisele admiring his muscled back. I am Han noting the knife in his ankle sheathe. I am Brian screaming. I am Mia suffering my first contractions, gasoline and blood spurting from my mouth as I begin to hyperventilate. I am Roman screaming. I am Tej screaming. I am pulling Shaw's pants off over his boots over his skin over his sister dying in her bed of spinal meningitis wheezing wheezing. I plunge a fist into his bloody asshole. He is screaming now. Somewhere cold and mountainous. Afghanistan. Wind scouring my skin.

I push deeper in. My hood folds back, supple as a newborn's skin. I flex skeins of tender muscle, newly grown, and my chassis parts like a pair of jaws. Not even a whisper as metal separates. It has been waiting for this. He is screaming. Crawling faster now, heedless of the broken glass that slices at him, pierces his abraded skin. I pin him flat with my other arms, longer than grown men, as long as my axles which are threaded now with miles and miles of nerves slipping like oil over the metal. He is screaming. He will scream for a long time, I think.

Some people don't understand that family is everything.

I open his mouth with one hand, yanking hard enough to dislocate his bottom jaw. "Your turn to say grace."

I'm going to have to show them what it means.

A Walking Tour of the First Act Car Chase in *Fast & Furious: Hobbs & Shaw*
Heather Davidson

Fast & Furious Presents: Hobbs & Shaw is not a good Fast & Furious movie. At the time of writing, *Hobbs & Shaw* is also the only Fast & Furious movie to completely ruin my wife's commute into her office for a week. That's because the film is part of a distinguished canon that includes the *Tetris* movie and that *Batgirl* movie Warner Bros. scrapped as a tax write-off, having been partially filmed in my hometown of Glasgow, Scotland.

While Luke Hobbs and Deckard Shaw and also Deckard Shaw's sister Hattie are meant to be chasing cybernetic villain Brixton Lore through the streets of central London at the end of the movie's first act, they are in fact driving in a loop around the same quarter-mile grid of roads in central Glasgow.

Reader, let's take a trip together down that quarter-mile, a quarter-mile at a time.

Our tour starts on the corner of St. Vincent Street and Hope Street, heading east. To be upfront with you, the tour will also end on St. Vincent Street, and will spend quite a lot of time in the middle on that road, too. Just as the main cast of *Hobbs & Shaw* teleport around 400 miles from London's financial district to begin this chase, I hope I can transport you from wherever you currently are, dear reader, to this spine of Glasgow's city centre.

Built in the early 1800s, as money was flooding into the city from the tobacco plantation owners who built their fortunes on the backs of enslaved people, St. Vincent Street's grand architecture is now mostly home to a wide array of perfectly fine fast-casual restaurants. In the movie, Hobbs and Shaw and also Shaw's sister Hattie speed past them in seconds, but we have the luxury of not being chased by Brixton Lore and his magical motorbike, so let's take a minute or two to relax. Perhaps we can even stop for lunch; we can live like Glasgow locals and contemplate the weight of centuries of oppression while eating a 6/10 vegan burger in a Gourmet Burger Kitchen with a Roman Doric doorway that was built when Queen Victoria had just ascended to the throne.

Hobbs and Shaw and Shaw's sister Hattie now continue up onto St. Vincent Place, heading towards George Square. We'll follow them as far as we can, but before they reach the square itself, we experience our first blip in the space-time continuum. The movie cuts to follow Lore on his motorbike, who is doing a pretty bad job chasing our protagonists given that he's back in London. We cut again to see through his perspective, which is once more the streets of Glasgow, rendered through a user interface so overwhelming it makes *Subway Surfers* #corecore TikTok look like the opening of *Tár*. One more cut and we're back following Shaw's McLaren where we started our chase on St. Vincent Street.

If you've retraced your steps back to St. Vincent Street, it's now time to turn back around and follow the exact same path we have already trod, crossing over Buchanan Street and up St. Vincent Place. This go-round, however, we will actually make it to George Square.

Now, if you stopped for lunch earlier when I suggested it, I'm sorry to say that you made a terrible mistake, for here is where our tour takes us past the George Square Greggs. To a dispassionate observer, Greggs is just a chain of bakeries, specialising in low-cost 'on-the-go' savoury food like sausage rolls and pasties. This description, though, comes nowhere near to conveying the vice-like grip Greggs has on the British psyche. The UK loves Greggs. There are more Greggs in the UK than Starbucks or McDonalds. Greggs has an ironic clothing line.

Greggs is a British institution, and you should never, ever see one in a *Fast & Furious* movie. The world of Fast & Furious is a world of backyard barbecues and awful tuna sandwiches at Toretto's Market & Cafe, not Yum Yums mass-produced in a business park outside Newcastle. Nobody puts on a Fast & Furious movie to watch an ex-MI6 agent with superpowers drive past the Greggs where I once saw a middle-aged TERF in a dinosaur costume queuing for a steak bake; we love the Fast & Furious franchise for its heart and its soul.

We cannot, however, hold this against Greggs itself. Stop off to pick up a vegan sausage roll or three, then turn around and head back down St. Vincent Street. Hobbs and Shaw and also Shaw's sister Hattie now teleport between shots to John Street, but we will have to walk, looping back to head through George Square and turning west to meet them.

While Lore takes another quick detour to London in order to drive his motorbike along a wall like it's 1999 and he just got out from seeing *The Matrix*, Hobbs and Shaw and, yes, also Shaw's sister Hattie spend the next section of this car chase driving in and out of Glasgow City Chambers. These are the headquarters of Glasgow City Council, whom we can thank for the existence of this deeply mid action sequence due to the creation of the Film Charter for the City of Glasgow in 1997.

The Film Charter sets out procedures that the council and its Film Office has to follow when dealing with TV and film productions, most notably that Glasgow council can't charge any production fees for filming in the city. In fact, in 2021 the council voted to give Warner Bros £150,000 as an incentive to shoot *Batgirl* in Glasgow. Central Glasgow now spends much of its time doubling for Gotham, London, or any number of American cities, and Glasgow's residents spend much of *their* time cussing out the council.

Good news! Hobbs and Shaw (and Hattie) eventually leave the City Chambers, which means we can too. Let's follow them past Katie's Bar on John Street, and try to pretend the one second of footage you see of pride flags hanging outside make up for the complete absence of homoerotic energy in this film.

We're back on St. Vincent Street one last time and, for true accuracy to the movie, you will want to make sure you walk up and down the street at least twice, maybe three times. Make sure to picture the cast of *Hobbs & Shaw* drifting under a couple of trucks as you do.

Our tour ends in the shadow of the Met Tower, now more often known as the "People Make Glasgow" tower, thanks to the slogan emblazoned across its iconic pink wrapping. Unfortunately, you may remember that the car chase we've just followed is meant to have taken place in London. In *Hobbs & Shaw*, therefore, we just see an indistinct blob of magenta, stripped through the power of CGI of any sense of place. This could be Glasgow; this could be London; this could be anywhere.

Brixton Lore crashes through a double-decker bus and our protagonists drive off into the distance. The movie enters its second act, and we don't see Glasgow again. Maybe we can stay here, though; *Hobbs & Shaw* can keep going on to wherever the next plot point takes it, and we can stay here, in Glasgow, and eat our sausage rolls.

Gender Envy
KJ

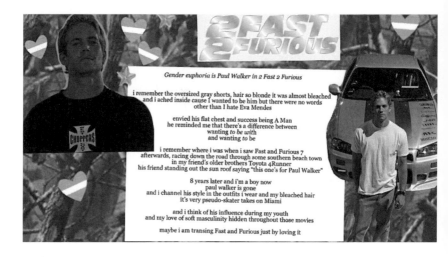

Gender euphoria is Paul Walker in 2 Fast 2 Furious

i remember the oversized gray shorts, hair so blonde it was almost bleached
and i ached inside cause I wanted to be him but there were no words
other than I hate Eva Mendes

envied his flat chest and success being A Man
he reminded me that there's a difference between
wanting *to be with*
and wanting *to be*

i remember where i was when i saw Fast and Furious 7
afterwards, racing down the road through some southern beach town
in my friend's older brothers Toyota 4Runner
his friend standing out the sun roof saying "this one's for Paul Walker"

8 years later and i'm a boy now
paul walker is gone
and i channel his style in the outfits i wear and my bleached hair
it's very pseudo-skater takes on Miami

and i think of his influence during my youth
and my love of soft masculinity hidden throughout those movies

maybe i am transing Fast and Furious just by loving it

The Fast and the Furious 69: TRANSmission (an FFT4TTTRPG)
Dakota Hommes

This is a game about imagining a future in which trans people still exist and Fast & Furious movies are still being made. You and your friends are directing the latest installment in the long-running driving franchise. This game can be played with any number of players. Everyone plays a character, whether hero or villain or something else.

Each player needs:
- a toy car (or an object made to represent a car)
- a d6

SET THE SCENE

To begin, describe the future when your film is set. Everyone should say at least one thing, such as an adjective or a way in which the world has changed. You could set your game in the place where you live, or as far away as outer space. Don't forget the soundtrack!

THE CREW

Describe your driver. Since it's the future, give them a body modification that comes with some kind of power or ability.

Examples: cybernetic angel wings, a literal scorpion tail, a body part that shoots lasers.

Explain how your character acquired their car. Describe your tricked-out ride for a bonus modifier. Examples: uses NOS (the energy drink), boat car, magnets. You can write all of this out on a notecard. Each car has a base HP of 6.

THE CHASE

Describe the kind of Chase you want to have. Examples: Race Wars, stealing a shipment of super HRT from a mega corporation, just going for a drive (but flirtatiously). Here's a fun idea: blowing up cop cars. When in doubt, I follow this pattern: race, then do crimes.

Draw an imaginary track on whatever surface you are using. I recommend laying pens and pencils to be the curb. You can use dice, notecards, and other objects to represent obstacles, other vehicles, JUMPS, etc. Describe what it all looks like. Add your cars as well.

Set the stakes. What are you racing for? A pink slip? A Drag Race championship title? The happiness of everyone you love? This may be different for each character.

Actions go in cycles. Everyone says what they want to do. (Rotate which player says their action first.) **You cannot change your action once you have said it aloud.**

"You make choices and you don't look back." - Han

Then everyone rolls dice at the same time and actions resolve in descending order. If your action uses either your character's or your car's special ability, you can add +1. If you are moving, your result is how many car lengths you can move. If you're attacking, it's how much damage you'll do.

If two players roll the same number, keep rolling until you get different results. The higher number resolves their action first, but both players keep their initial number for damage or distance.

Here's an example of a turn:

Everyone says what they want to do.
Dom: *I'm gonna hit Brian's car with my Big Fist. +1*
Brian: *I'm going to make this jump to avoid Dom.*
Jesse: *I'm going to go fast towards the finish line.*
They roll dice.
Results: *D = 2+1=3, B = 3, J = 6*
Dom and Brian roll again. Dom gets a 2 and Brian gets a 4.
Jesse goes fast and moves six car lengths. Brian hits the jump and narrowly avoids a hit from Dom's big fist that would have been 3 damage.

Show the actions with your cars. If a player drifts, they can earn a Drift Point. Drift Points can be spent to perform an action instantly without having to roll that turn, or to do something extra ridiculous.

Repeat until the Chase reaches a conclusion.

CONVERSATION

After a Chase, you should debrief. Have your characters discuss the impact of the Chase's outcome. You can also use this time to set up the next Chase. A feature movie should have about 2-3 Chases. A good way to wrap up a movie is by eating a meal in the backyard and drinking a Corona.

WEAR A SEATBELT

It's a good idea to include some kind of safety tool in your game. I recommend using an X card (created by John Stavropoulos: tinyurl.com/x-card-rpg) that players can touch or raise if they feel uncomfortable with the content of the story.

CREDITS

Thank you to Emily B., Yael Jacobs, and Wing Mui for playtesting this game. Special thanks to Phoenix Comics and Games.

Faster & Even More Furious: A Demo Derby Driver's Perspective
Jameson Alea

Like many of us, I deeply appreciate the Fast franchise for a number of reasons. But one of my reasons is a little unusual: it turned me into a bit of a race car driver myself.

I made my driving debut in September 2022, at a demolition derby-style event called CRASH-A-RAMA in rural upstate New York. My foray into demolition derby was partially inspired by my love of these movies, and I thought it would be a fitting tribute to revisit the classic 2 *Fast* 2 *Furious* and its beloved demo derby scene, and see how it stacks up to my experience on the real dirt track.

In the beginning of *2F2F*, Brian returns to California, hoping to recruit his old friend Roman to help track down a drug dealer for the FBI. He finds Roman driving in the demolition derby at "Barstow Speedway," which actually bears more than a passing resemblance to Holland Speedway, where I made my driving debut. I mean, all you really need is a spot in kinda the middle of nowhere, some bleacher-style seats, maybe a couple of food trucks, and a handful of drivers willing to put in the work to make their cars look *mean*. Because first things first, yes, people do give their cars delightfully crappy and colorful paint jobs.

Here's a photo of me with my car, which I decorated in honor of my Family, the Bills Mafia. (You can't tell from the photo, but the stripes are in Buffalo Bills zubaz colors: white, blue and red.) I think this is important to share, both because you can't fully appreciate the story without knowing what the car looks like, and also because I don't want to risk anyone thinking that I'm just doing a bit.

Unfortunately, the similarities between Roman's derby and my Crash-a-Rama start to deteriorate after that. I get the sense that Roman and his pals at Barstow Speedway are doing this shit *all the time*. There's demo derby just casually going on in the middle of the afternoon, and while the fans in attendance are enthusiastic, the stands aren't exactly packed. On the other hand, Crash-a-Rama is an *event* that draws a crowd. It happens only twice a year, and you better not forget to pick up your advance tickets from Napa Auto Parts because this shit is going to *sell out*.

Admittedly, Crash-a-Rama is a more elaborate affair where demo derby is only one of a number of similarly-high-impact competitions. The schedule is rounded out with a bunch of races designed to maximize dramatic crashes: the flagpole race, where drivers loop around a flagpole each lap in the face of oncoming traffic; the boat and trailer race, where each racer drags a 16-foot boat behind their car like the safe in *Fast Five*; and of course the classic "school bus figure 8," which is exactly what it sounds like and requires no further explanation.

Still, the overall vibe is similar. Okay, I've never seen a car crash into the stands before, but someone was ejected for getting pissed off and driving right through the pit and running over the firetruck's hose. The dude in the movie who kicked out his own windshield from inside the car definitely brought me back to watching some guy frantically kicking at his own tail lights and pulling them out with his hands on the track during a red flag because tail lights aren't allowed, dude, how'd they even let you out here with those still in? And the way the other audience members just sat back and watched as Brian and Roman beat the shit out of each other reminded me of a fight that broke out between two drivers right on the track after the school bus race. I would have thought it was part of the show if I wasn't part of the show myself, but I suppose it would have become clear when the cops showed up. (I absolutely swear to you that I'm not making any of this up.)

The Barstow demolition derby is only a short scene near the beginning of *2F2F*, but as I continued to enjoy this 2003 masterpiece, I realized that it's not even the scene *in this movie* that reminded me the most of my derby experience. That honor actually goes to a set piece in the finale that happens to be one of my favorite set pieces in the entire franchise: Brian and Roman, in hot pursuit by the cops, drive their souped up cars into a concrete warehouse and close up the door behind them. There's a long, tense moment as police surround the building. It's not clear what they're doing in there, or who will make the first move. And then the warehouse doors open... and cars start pouring out. Hundreds of them. Like they just keep coming, for way longer than you'd expect. A cop watching from above in a helicopter says, "holy shit." There are cars everywhere and it is madness.

Now, let me stop and tell you about the main event at Crash-a-Rama: the Enduro Race. On paper, the Enduro sounds like the *least* crazy event in the lineup. Race for an hour, no special caveats, and whoever does the most laps is the winner. Easy enough, right? Seventy-two drivers, including me, entered the Enduro—and I'm going to need you to stop and try to picture 72 cars racing at the same time on a track that's three-eighths of a mile long.

It would be hard to overstate just how many fucking cars that is. It was a bloodbath, and only 18 of those original 72 cars were still running at the end of an hour. I'd like to put an image in your head of what it's like to see that many cars racing that close together, but legitimately the best approximation I can think of is, "it's like that scene at the end of *2 Fast 2 Furious* where all the cars come pouring out of the warehouse."

(If you were wondering, I was one of those 18 surviving cars! I completed the fewest laps of the finishers, but hey, 54 cars didn't even finish. Unlike in *2F2F*, I didn't get to crash into any cop cars, which is unfortunate. But I *did* do the boat and trailer race, so actually I did crash directly through a boat! Nobody was shooting at me, but the boat I drove into was smaller and there wasn't much of it left afterwards.)

While the *actual* demolition derby at Barstow Speedway wasn't a great reflection of my experience as a real life driver, somehow the entire film *2 Fast 2 Furious* as a whole... kind of was, actually. I think it's because the Fast franchise is really just about the love of driving and of our friends that we know through driving, and I can certainly relate to that now. I'll leave you with one last thing I can't quite relate to: clearly I live my life *three-eighths* of a mile at a time.

By Milo   *Editors note: This isn't fanfic. Everything on this page is true!*

The Fast and the Haikurious
Miche Devey

The Fast and the Furious

How is the tuna?
Only a cop would ask that
The tuna is crap

2 Fast 2 Furious

Nissan Skyline go
Undercover to clear name
No Vin Diesel, what?

Tokyo Drift

Southern kid abroad
Learns to slide car around, wow
No wax on, wax off

Fast & Furious

Bri, still a buster
Only pussies run nitro
Oh no, not Letty

Fast Five

It's a heist this time
Dragging a vault around town
Wait, is that Letty?

Fast & Furious 6

Shot in my city
Amnesia is a hassle
Full pardons all 'round

Furious 7

Brian is retired
Goodbye, Paul, we'll miss you so
Tears fall in the sand

The Fate of the Furious

Nuclear football
Elena deserved better
Welcome baby Bri

F9

Han is not dead, yay!
Magnets — they don't work like that
A car went to space

Jason Statham Will Call My Dad A Pussy In *Fast 12*
Malachi

I fucking hate cars. I hate cars because on November 28, 2016, my father was riding his scooter to work when a woman used her SUV to kill him (not on purpose so it's not a big deal though, she was just distracted, no biggie). His murder made my "im just a gay who can't drive" bit into, annoyingly, something that feels like a moral imperative for me.

I also love a dumb action movie, and lack any sense, which is why, just a few months after a woman killed my dad with her car, I went to go see the *F8 of the Furious*. I don't remember much about it except realizing from the first car crash that I was dissociating, and thinking "this was a mistake" as I sat there imagining the agony my dad felt as he died for two hours and 16 minutes. I was so completely gone that when the friend I was sitting next to—who was profoundly blammo from a work function—vomited into a cup she found on the floor, I did not notice a thing.

Because I'm an idiot, that experience didn't stop me from watching all the movies again, and even seeing *Hobbs & Shaw*, which is absolute detritus, in the theater. Rewatching all of the Fast and the Furious was a bit like exposure therapy if the prescribing psychiatrist (me) was an absolute moron (I am). I guess it worked though, because, at some point, I became able to keep my eyes open for most of a crash scene; and when Letty, and then Han, inexplicably survived, the crashes themselves became a pure fantasy.

In the world of Fast, if you're morally good, death is impermanent, especially if it's in a car crash. I mean, they managed to keep Paul Walker alive after he literally died in an actual car crash. In Fast, if you are good, you can survive anything except jet wheels.

I don't think that the fantasy is good for the world, but at this point, the crashes in Fast are an art form; they're a display of pyro; they're a signifier for drama. Now, I don't disassociate for the whole movie—when I see a crash, I just have a moment when I think, "Oh, just like how my daddy died." And then I keep going, because the crash that killed him was normal, mundane, boring; it wasn't newsworthy; it wasn't stupid art like in Fast; it was just a man being crushed to death under an SUV on his way to work. In Fast, nobody that good goes out that way.

I know that the fantasy is bad, but sometimes I want to live in it. In the world of *Fast*, I think, my dad is still alive, and one day, on the streets of Atlanta, where presumably he's come to steal the Olympic flame or a briefcase of diseases (?) from the CDC, Jason Statham swerves around my dad while chasing Dom and shouts, "Who is this pussy riding a Vespa?"

Later, my dad calls me and says, "Willie, you won't believe what happened to me today: this British asshole nearly ran me off the road chasing a little bald man in an Impala!" and then he tells me about what he bought at the farmers' market. In the world of Fast, this is nothing special, and I can call my dad whenever I want, because he was good, so he lived.

An Ode to X
SamuelAnimates

X is an icon. X is a symbol. X is the signifier and the signified. X is the film crew and X is the main character and X is carrying the bagels from craft services. X is the main character in the penultimate installment of the internationally acclaimed Fast & Furious film series: Fast X. X is a letter. And sometimes a number. And sometimes a placeholder.

X for X-treme. X for X-citing. 2 X, 2 Xurious.

X X, X Xxxxxx. X-it. X-plainable. X-iled. X-tenuating circumstances.

Hot days. Cold nights. Warm seat cool breeze fast car go fast X dazzle silver screen X beauty X brains X face X style. Hair perfectly tousled from a high speed chase and focus unbroken and pace of breathing unchanged and beaming moonlight and towering buildings and blurry lines and the road is xyrs but also it's all of ours and also none of ours and maybe somehow the city's as a public good? But also this image of it most definitely belongs to Universal Pictures. X-hilarating.

X lives in the moment of silence at the front of the security line, when someone wants to refer to zir as "sir" or "ma'am" but then hesitates. In the quotation marks around "this stuff." Always a wink and a laugh. Always a scowl and an exit. Always a thing. Always not a big deal, really. Never a burden. Never burdened. Cool-tempered yet hot-headed. Yes and no. And no but yes. And yes, but we're not going to do anything about it. And no but yes, but no, and yes, but just give us 6 or 7 or 10 years, that's all.

X doesn't wait in line in the basement for the only gender-inclusive toilet in the building. X is the line. X is two lines. X is the concept of a line. X is the cartesian coordinate system. X is X and X is Y.

X is perfect with numbers and even better with words. Witty banter fueled by iced coffee and the need for speed. Eir body is all hot glue gun holsters and secret sewing kit compartments. Why? Because they FASTEN FURIOUS. A frayed edge of synthetic fabric? Melted down. A loose button? Reattached. A misshapen piece of fast fashion that's still better than trying on clothes in the store? Belted for the gods. As good as they are with numbers and words and fashion, X is even better at driving.

X feels most like X when X is in motion. When you were feuding with Vin Diesel, X was driving. When you kiss and make up with Vin Diesel, X will be driving. One day, about 10 billion years from now, when you hold Vin Diesel's hand and stare lovingly into each other's teary eyes as the sun incinerates the earth for its closing number, X will STILL. BE. DRIVING.

X gets shit done all day and then turns off their phone 2 hours before bedtime. X drinks water and stretches. X loves doctors and doctors love X. X has never had a frightening encounter on the train and never had a discouraging experience in an office. You turn to look at X and strike up a conversation fae're not interested in, but in the blink of an eye X is already gone. X screams into the void and knocks down skyscrapers and breathes fire and knocks out the electric lines and eats helicopters because WHAT PART OF "FAST" AND "FURIOUS" DO YOU NOT UNDERSTAND?

XTERIOR. INTERSECTION – DAY. Three cars, side by side, RUMBLE with power. Dominic and Brian and X look at each other from the warmth of their driver's seats. X: "We used to race here in high school, remember? That stoplight up there is a quarter-mile from here." Between their current intersection and the stoplight is a railroad crossing. To the left, an exciting distance away, is a train, moving at an exciting speed.

X: "When that stop light turns, I'm gonna go for it and never look back. I wanted to say goodbye now, since I'm going to beat that train and you two won't."
Brian and Dominic: "So you're just going to drive away from all your problems?"
X: "All my problems? All I see here is you two."
Brian and Dominic: "We understand."

They don't, though. But they believe they do, and even though the three of them are all beyond bullshitting with each other, X doesn't want to get into it. So X just winks at Dominic and smiles. The stoplight turns green, and all three cars are off.

Three hands clutch gear shifters. Three feet put three pedals to three floors. Three engines roar. And one car pulls ahead. The screen is a rapid-fire montage of metal and skin and rubber and road. The two rear cars nearly catch up to the other as the train barrels ahead. As the two rear cars maneuver to sandwich the other in, it lunges forward. The two rear cars bump into each other at top speed, swerving out of control and screeching to a halt as the crossbucks lower on either side of the tracks. X barrels forward, faster than ever as time slows down to a halt. X can hear individual molecules of gas in the combustion engine, speaking to them, guiding them on their path through the car's arteries. The road is singing and X is harmonizing with it, a song from a childhood that feels now like someone else's dream. Brian and Dominic step out of their cars and watch as X pulls ahead of the railroad crossing just in time, busting through the crossbucks with a loud CRACK, headed to destinations unknown. They know X will be over the horizon by the time the train clears the tracks, and the two of them will still be standing on the side of the road.

The Cipher Cut
aj castle

This essay is part love letter, part criticism, part comparative analysis that stems from and is completely devoted to Cipher's bowl cut from *F9: The Fast Saga*. Cipher's bowl cut, as an object of analysis, can be taken as literal (i.e., just a haircut), but I am interested in the bowl cut as both a symbol of greater queer tension and a comparative link between seemingly unrelated films. The bowl cut as the hairstyle of a high-tech supervillain surfaces a certain level of postmodern gender tension in reflection to the modern anti-hero, Dominic Toretto, and his cars. The epitome of modern masculinity, Dom is a master of the technologies of modernity represented by the fast car, and leads a universally good (well, in *F9*) Robin Hood existence in service of the state. Dom is a hero, his own man, the provider for his family, and his greatest threat is the postmodern tech bro—even more so, a postmodern tech master that pushes the boundaries of gender and masculinity.

Cipher's representation potential is neither appropriately masculine nor feminine. Cipher codes and is queer-coded. Her character arc is intentionally problematic and dissonant. We, the audience, are supposed to hate her and everything she could possibly represent. She has access to all information, no boundaries, and deals in access to secrets. If the foundation of the modern state rests on a masculine cisheteropatriarchy, then Cipher's obsessive intent to destroy the state is to shake that foundation in a way that I understand to be postmodern. As an aesthetic and a thought tradition, postmodernism is frustrating and full of contradictions, taking ideas and objects out of time and marking them for commercialization or commodification. Cipher's ability to transcend boundaries includes the rigid categories of socially constructed gender; her irreversible damage hole is self-filling, a kinetic sand mess of gender fluidity, symbolized and mythologized by a bowl cut. Cipher heralds the end of the modern man, Dom. Yet, the modern man holds faithful to the technologies of his modern identity: cars, family, and finite masculinity, and emerges somewhat victorious, although the threat of bowl cut postmodernism continues to loom.

Cipher's bowl cut surfaces that *F9* is nothing more than a live-action translation of *Despicable Me*. Cipher is a direct translation of the animated villain, Vector. We hate them and their silly bowl cuts because whatever Cipher/Vector does it is always just a little bit better, a little bit smarter, and a little bit higher tech than our anti-hero Dom/Gru. (I mean, Cipher also killed Dom's kid's mother, but that was a different movie). And if we were ever in doubt of our plot and pattern recognition skills, this realization is confirmed through the meta-discourse easter egg in the film's conclusion. After the film has essentially ended, all the explosions have exploded, and we have been dutifully reminded of the importance of family, we are given a scene in which Tej and Roman float in space near what can be assumed to be the International Space Station. A Russian astronaut looks at the yellow, puffy-suited Tej and Roman and says, "Why do they look like...minions?," all but necessitating a scene where Cipher moon walks out of her plastic cell, and exclaims, "I'm Cipher!" before slamming a Big Gulp and plotting once again to steal the moon.

Yet, Cipher is completely dehumanized (often signaling postmodernism), a shiny object in a literal plastic box. Even the dialogue between Cipher and the other villains sounds like it was written by a poorly funded chatbot: awkward, racist, fraught with tension. Cipher is denied complex personhood because granting this particular villain complex personhood would detract from barely existent complexity within the heroes. It is this very flattening that sparked my sense of déjà vu and linked *F9* to *Despicable Me* well before the minion denouement. The only way forward—and hopefully, the plot of *Fast X*—is for our modern anti-hero and our postmodern tech villain to join forces against the state, finally realizing that Mr. Nobody is the true villain… but keeping the bowl cut.

3 Times Brian O'Conner Almost Had Dominic Toretto
Dizzy

August 12th, 2001. Los Angeles, California.

"Let me give you a massage, Dom," Letty said, a restraining hand on Dom's shoulder. His knuckles were white, clenched into fists, but he relented, allowing the force of his gaze to slip off of Vince. Letty pulled Dom up the stairs by his hand, and Brian waited as long as he could before following.

Just looking for the bathroom, that's all. Brian could almost convince himself, tip-toeing up the stairs to the unfamiliar house and nudging the doors in the hallway open one-by-one, just enough that he could see through the crack in the door. His breath caught in his throat when he found the door he was looking for—no, the bathroom, he was just looking for the bathroom—and saw Letty on her knees at the foot of the bed. Dom's cock was even bigger than he'd imagined, a thick slab of meat rock-hard between his thighs. Letty let out a low sigh, her eyes rolling back just enough to meet Dom's.

"Massage?" Dom's voice was a low rumble, gravely and warm, the sharpness he'd directed at Vince bled out.

"What, like I'm gonna say 'let me take you upstairs and suck you off' in front of your sister and the new kid?'"

Dom's fingers tangled up in Letty's hair, made a loose fist and pulled her in closer. Her lips closed around the head of his cock, moan turning into a muffled buzz as he rolled his hips up off the bed to slide slowly across her tongue. Brian's heart pounded somewhere high up in his chest, his cheeks flushed. He knew he was on precarious ground with Dom's crew, and getting caught spying on the boss and his girlfriend wouldn't do much to improve his standing, but he couldn't help it. Letty's lips stretched out into an 'O', her head bobbing in slow, steady rhythm. Dom's fingers were still in her hair, but he was laid out flat on the bed, eyes on the ceiling. Brian imagined that thick dick wedging his jaw open, the taste of pre-cum on his tongue, a line of drool dripping down his chin and splattering on the floor between his knees...

Somehow Brian managed to tear himself away, stumble down the hallway to the bathroom. He leaned his head against the wall it shared with Dom's bedroom, listening to Dom's muffled groans until someone knocked on the door, snapping him out of his reverie. He turned on the taps and managed to let out a "One second!" in a voice that he hoped wouldn't betray the flush in his cheeks. "One second, just..."

June 16th, 2002. Somewhere in Arizona.

The sun beat down orange-yellow and hot on the hood of a Nissan Skyline GT-R R34, and Brian O'Conner was thinking of Dom. The car was idling somewhere off I-10 – a nowhere stretch of highway – and with the windows down the heat was stifling, sweat beading

68

on Brian's neck and rolling down to the crag of his collarbones. It was too hot for any shirt at all, much less the three-sizes-too-large t-shirts that made up 90% of his wardrobe. Brian couldn't help but imagine Dom in one of his shirts, the oversized T's Brian would swim in stretched tight over Dom's massive frame, silver cross dangling between his outsized pectorals. Brian's thumb hooked under the waistband of his jeans, relieving some of the pressure there as he imagined tracing the lines of Dom's chest, down towards his abs.

Condensation from the radiator sizzled audibly under the hood of Brian's Skyline as he pictured pressing his lips to Dom's ribs, tracing the lines under each one with his fingertips as he worked his way down towards his abs. Every muscle there was so clearly defined; Brian's cock was hard against his palm as he recalled the way Dom's muscles rippled just under the skin when he peeled out of his undershirt in the too-hot auto-shop where they met. Every inch of Dom was too big to be believed; they were the same height but Brian felt dwarfed by him, outsized and outclassed.

Brian found the jock strap in the passenger's seat with his free hand, the only reminder he had from Dom. He brought it up to his nose and breathed deep, imagining what it would be like if he could drink in that powerful, masculine musk straight from the source. He let out a low groan as he pictured Dom's heavy balls, burying his face in them to worship them with his tongue. It was too much, too much; with one more deep inhale Brian came, his cock twitching in his hand as he shot jet after jet of spunk onto his stomach, pearlescent slime pooling in his bellybutton.

January 9th, 2006. London, England.

Brian couldn't help but groan as Mia pulled out of him, leaving him suddenly, achingly empty. His thighs and upturned ass cold without her body pressed up against him. He rolled his hips against the bed, stiff cock grinding against the sheets. "Did... did I do something wrong?" He looked over his shoulder at his wife, expecting to see her ready to punish him for some imagined slight.

"You said his name," Mia said, pulling away from him to stand at the foot of the bed. "Again."

Brian's breath came out of him in a low whoosh. He was still desperately hard, the ropes around his wrists creaking as he moved to touch himself and came up short. "I didn't, I must've said..."

Before the stammered sentence was halfway out of his mouth, Mia's hand came down hard on his ass, the sharp crack and Brian's yelp echoing in their small bedroom. Another spank followed the first, his yelp drawing out into a slow whine.

"You did," Mia said, her voice firm. Brian's head swam, too endorphin-drunk to tell if she was actually angry or not.

"Are y—" He barely got the first word out before she hit him again, a sharp slap on his face that turned his flushed cheeks even pinker.

"Did I say you could talk?" Brian's jaw clicked shut, and he shook his head, hips twitching to rub himself against the bed, desperate for any stimulation. He knew Mia could see him do it, hoped she would let it slide. "Good. Keep your fucking mouth shut."

He managed it for a moment, teeth catching his lower lip, fingers making knots of the sheets under his bound hands. He kept his mouth shut as Mia settled between his legs again, pushing his thighs a little further apart with her knees. He bit his lip as she rolled her hips forward, slick, hard cock sliding aimlessly between his cheeks before she wrapped her hand around it and guided herself towards his well-fucked hole. Only a tiny whimper parted his lips as she pressed forward, hips twitching back towards her. When Brian's body gives way to her, suddenly filled up again with her thick length, he couldn't help but let out a deep, low moan, jaw hanging open and tongue lolling out of his mouth. Mia panted into his ear as she drove her hips forward, hilting herself in her husband's needy asshole.

"Now," she hissed, pulling his head back by his hair, "Call me Dom."

*Artist statement on pg 145

Ready 2 Race
Tehya

WHAT'S YOUR

fast and furious

NAME?

last digit of phone number:

0: Quarter-Mile
1: King/Queen
2: Hybrid
3: Ultra
4: VroomVroom
5: Sexy
6: Reckless
7: Lil
8: Lucky
9: Macho

sun sign:

Aries: Nas
Taurus: Crime
Gemini: Carwash
Cancer: Tuna
Leo: Drift
Virgo: Fuego
Libra: Diesel
Scorpio: Rumble
Sagittarius: Ride or Die
Capricorn: Orbit
Aquarius: 2Fast
Pisces: Baby

favorite transportation:

Car: Brother/Sister
Truck: Lane Switcha
Train: Racer
Boat: Brian

Bus: Daddy/Mommy
Motorcycle: Boss
Helicopter: Carwreck
Rocket: Freak

Submarine: Outlaw
UFO: Snack
Bicycle: Muscle
Jet: Corona

Fast vs Furious: Our Favorite Films
Contributor Collective

Which Fast & Furious film reigns supreme? We asked our contributors to make the case for their favorite Fast flicks, and compiled the highlights for your viewing pleasure.

The Fast and the Furious (3 votes)

"It's the purest distillation of early 2000s energy and profound homoeroticism" - *Max T*

2 Fast 2 Furious (6 votes)

"We love the collective action scene where all the cars come out of the garage at once! Community working together!" - *Ezra & Nettle*

"Suki!" - *AA & AK*

"The '2 _____ 2_____' format really changed the game" - *Samuel*

Tokyo Drift (6 votes)

"It has the best vibes. Twink. The opening credits music. Han being peak Han. The best actual driving and car culture. It's kind of a samurai movie. I cry at the end when Dom shows up" - *Mckenzee*

"Tokyo Drift is underrated with its classic fish-out-of-water tale, a solid soundtrack through-and-through, and Han being so damn cool they restructured canon entirely to bless us with more of him. (Sorry, Rusty Ryan, Han's been crowned the ultimate constantly-snacking king.) While there are a ton of racial dynamics to unpack, I love that it subverts--and textually calls out--the hot Asian girlfriend trope, and Sean is a good driver who actually spends time learning to do a whole different style of racing. Plus, it's still rare to see an action movie starring someone with a Southern regional accent. Most importantly though, it made me want to learn how to do cool driving shit in a way no other Fast movie has" - *Kim*

"It's an actual movie" - *Gretchen*

Fast & Furious (5 votes)

"Putting a boosted RB26DET in a vintage mustang" - *Adrian*

"I know it's an unconventional choice, but I love how homoerotic this movie is and I think the emotional storylines are actually pretty well done? Also, Vin Diesel drives a car into someone and then says 'pussy' at their corpse, which is an iconic moment" - *Keely*

"The Rock ruined the franchise! Gun fights are so uncool compared to car racing" - *Malachi*

Fast Five (8 votes)

"They drag a VAULT through RIO" - *Heather*

"SWINGING THE VAULT AROUND LIKE A HUGE MACE" - *Lillie*

"It's *Ocean's Eleven*. Also, when the Rock is chasing them, he instructs his team, 'Don't ever, *ever* let them get into cars'" - *Tuck*

Fast & Furious 6 (no votes)

Furious 7 (6 votes)

"THE APOTHEOSIS of What They Are Are Trying to Do" - *Mattie*

"The Rock gets so mad he flexes a plaster cast off his arm and says, 'Daddy has to go to work'" - *Jillian*

"You can really feel how much they love each other in this one, ya know? And the Paul Walker tribute just wrecks me every time" - *Al*

"Every time I watch it I cry even harder at the goddamn See You Again shit!!!! That's literally the only reason!!" - *Max R*

The Fate of the Furious (no votes)

Hobbs & Shaw (1 vote)

"Okay, so bear with me because I actually really meditated on this question for some reason, lol. Whenever I take a minute to think about which FF movie is my favorite, my brain always goes to Hobbs & Shaw, and it's certainly a fun and funny movie that I really like a lot, but I think the reason that I think of it as my FAVORITE is because the mainline movies kind of blend together in my head a lot. When I think of my favorite stuff from the mainline movies, I tend to think about individual setpieces: I like the scene at the end of 2 where all the cars come out of the garage to confuse the cops. I like the bank vault chase in 5. I like the car jumping between the buildings in 7, but I had to look up if that happened in 7 or 8 because I didn't remember. So I don't really think that I think about the movies in terms of individual stories, but more like one big whole that has pieces I like scattered all throughout it. But *Hobbs & Shaw* feels more like one movie that goes together in my head that I can point at and say 'That one! I love that movie!'" - *Jameson*

F9 (3 votes)

"Han's back! Magnets! Space! But also, I think the presented relationship dynamics between Dom, Letty, and Dom's kid with Elsa saw the franchise move into family dynamics that you don't always see. The compersion Letty has for Dom (or at least, the compersion I read into the text) always warms my heart" - *Ponders*

"Because they went to space, duh" - *Lee*

Declined to answer (6 votes)

"I have never seen a fast film. Please don't be furious" - *Skylar*

Little Tokyo Retrofit
Kim Kuzuri

I am painstakingly rebuilt Japanese
American muscle—sculpted, sun-warmed, greased and glistening.
A
shrine to sweat and leather with a gutter roar, a glitter snarl—a
versatile
hard top dragster
who has never known when to let off the gas; Drift on, I tell myself,
when gendered
by pedestrian passersby. Focus on the horizon where the markers
for passing dissolve,
consumed by a gasoline-fume blur. Iridescent. Incandescent.
There is no speed limit but my own now. I set the terms of this
race, where
I lead and I chase and I know
Each mile is victory in a frame welded together by spit and tears,
the kindness of dykes and daddies and candy ass queers. The only
finish line
        to cruise towards? Freedom

And if the parts of me that still don't know how to take up space or
span the lanes of
generational trauma imported into my bones whisper
                                        すみません

Drift on, I'll tell myself.
Drift on.
Your roots span oceans. You can rewrite where you belong.
There's more family to love (you)
around the bend.

Missing in Action
Marina Crustacean

*Artist statement on pg 146

My Day of Speed and Anger

Marina Crustacean

Two days after my 22nd birthday, I woke up at 4:20 in the morning, made some oatmeal, and proceeded to watch every *Fast & Furious* movie released to date in just under 24 hours. This included Fasts 1 through 9, the six-minute prelude to *2 Fast 2 Furious*, the short film *Los Bandoleros* (written and directed by Vin Diesel), and the spin-off *Hobbs & Shaw*, the only piece of F&F media I had seen previously.

As any reasonable person might assume, this is not a very good way to introduce yourself to a series. The Fast & Furious franchise is built on repeated elements and motifs: the concept of "family," for example, and also women's asses. Absorbed over time, this is fine, but condensed together, it can get really tiring when every movie is about the exact same thing (except for *Fast 3*, which is about how drifting is super cool).

Watching it all in one chunk produces reference hell. It has been drilled into my brain that Roman is hungry, and that Dom lives his life one quarter-mile at a time. "Remember when this crazy thing from the previous movies happened?" Yes, I do remember. I saw it right after lunch. Character moments lose their luster, too; Letty dies, comes back amnesic, and then regains her memory within about 7 hours, while Han gets resurrected about 5 hours after his last appearance in *Fast 6*. Dom's charger is destroyed 4 times, and his necklace gets passed around so much it makes you dizzy.

Many kinds of shots see repeated use—cars flipping in the air, thumbs on turbo buttons, Vin Diesel's sad face—but even some niche shots still occur several times over the course of the series. Fasts 1, 3, and 4 all show women kissing each other to indicate a cool party (nice?), while the climaxes of 5 and 6 both contain a shot of a small child watching the action from inside a bus, something you would only notice watching them back-to-back.

The question begs to be asked: why did I even do this?

In *Fast 8*, there's a scene where a bunch of cars burst out of a parking garage and rain down into the street from above. They fill the frame with this vehicular mass, more cars piling in from the top and the sides, their successive impacts making the rest of the wreck jiggle like some sort of absurd physics simulation. The scene is relevant to the plot, of course, but its main value lies in the spectacle, and the sheer volume of crunched metal that accretes in front of the camera.

The F&F franchise similarly forms a kind of massive homogenized car slurry, and there is an accompanying sense that you can only truly experience it as one big whole. Watching them separately, you see 10 Fast and Furious movies, 1 short film, and 1 DVD bonus; together, you see Fast & Furious.

Ick, okay, forget about the try-hard metaphor; obviously, there's another reason. While the Fast & Furious franchise may be primarily about heists, ludicrous (Ludacris?) action set-pieces, and—as Dom will not let anyone forget—family, it's also about speed.

And I bet no one else has seen it faster than me.

Dominic Gaudium Est
Alyssa Grimley

Despite my Catholic upbringing, I never really understood the urge to proselytize. What other people believed was their business and wasn't any of mine. The closest thing to a fiery evangelical passion I had was reserved for movies.

The Sacred Texts: The entries on the AFI top 100 list.
The Holy Relics: Criterion Collection DVD box sets.
The Sermon on the Mount: Anything by Roger Ebert.
The Divine Reward: The Oscar.

I cared about movies more than just about anything and took them deathly seriously. If it wasn't directed by Christopher Nolan or nominated for 11 Oscars, it wasn't worth my time. Sure, I liked other kinds of movies, but in my mind, only "serious" movies deserved to be taken seriously.

I might have remained on that crooked path if a college friend hadn't shown me the light. This friend and I bonded over our love of film and spent much of our time together curating themed movie nights—the more esoteric and tenuous the theme, the better. (A standout: U.S. Marshal Night, featuring *Shutter Island* and the pilot episode of *Justified*).

One night, this friend sat me down and asked me a question. Had I heard the good word of Dominic Toretto? Had I found Family? (He'd just seen *Furious 7* and was a changed man. His eyes shone with fervor as he spoke.)

Of course I'd heard of F&F, but I assumed it had nothing to offer me. When I told my friend as much, he made me a promise: if I embarked on this road with him and gave these dumb movies a chance, he personally guaranteed that I'd be moved to tears by the end.

I was skeptical but had faith in my friend. We made a covenant right then and there and started drafting our most ambitious movie night yet. So powerful was his religious ecstasy that he convinced me to marathon all seven films over the course of two days. My journey had begun.

Fueled by Tollhouse cookies, sausage biscuits, and a 24-pack of Corona, together we discovered that neither of us really liked Corona (sorry, Vin). Also, the promise he made to me came true. I was a blubbering mess by the last scene of *Furious 7*. I was changed.

Now, were these movies *good*? I mean, not by Scorsese standards. But they're extremely good at being what they are: an extended series of physics-defying set pieces propped up by an endearing, ever-growing cast of characters with a self-imposed directive to up the camp level with every installment. (Through Dom, all things are possible. A beefy man can flex out of a cast or stomp through a parking garage floor. A car, driven with enough heart and well-timed one-liners, can indeed fly. And, so long as your crew has a designated "tech guy," a car can absolutely go to space).

Once I'd seen the light, I realized that working to classify F&F as "good" or "bad" was not only a waste of time but also entirely beside the point. These movies, if you opened your heart to the experience of them, were pure, distilled joy. And, following my baptism by Corona into the Fast Family, I came to realize that the NOS-fueled joy of this franchise only compounded the more I shared it with others.

Exhibit A: It's 2019 and I've started a new job. I had become fast friends with the coworker I share an office with. After I gush about F&F to her, she devours the films over the course of a few days, like I did. She sends me her live reactions via Snapchat, delightedly documenting the gayest moments (Brian is hilariously quick to abandon his dreams of becoming a respectable federal agent once he meets a certain charming, gravelly-voiced outlaw). I relive the joy of my initiation into the Family as she experiences it all for the first time. I gift her the rubber tire-shaped DVD box set for Hanukkah, which comes in clutch for future movie nights.

Exhibit B: It's 2020 and I'm wracked with existential angst pretty much 24/7. I tell a friend who would eventually become my partner about these movies and he, too, diligently consumes them in quick succession. We live in different states and start watching TV shows and movies on video calls together. One night, I'm feeling particularly anxious about the world as I join him on a call. When his video connects, he's dressed in a bald cap, wife beater, sunglasses, and cross necklace—a surprise Dom cosplay to make me smile. It works. I whoop with joyous laughter and fall in love with him a little more.

Realizing how in the dark I was about this franchise helped me realize how much growing I had to do. And it turned out that my deconstruction of one restrictive binary (that of "good" and "bad" movies) coincided with another. Over time, I gradually grew more comfortable and confident with embracing my nonbinary identity and realized that what I'd built up in my mind as so stark and so important to maintain was much larger, messier, and so much more beautifully complicated than I'd originally believed.

The more I grow into myself, the hazier and smaller my film bro self becomes in the rear-view mirror. Those Oscar-winning movies I dutifully consumed used to make up such an integral part of who I was that I took every dismissal of one of these sacred texts as blasphemy. I realize now how deeply rooted in insecurity and the need for approval that mindset was.

Discovering, loving, and sharing this franchise (and myself) with others has been such a wildly different experience—maybe even the opposite experience—than self-policing myself into who I thought I should be. It's nourishing, welcoming—an open invitation to learn and grow rather than an ongoing test to constantly worry about failing. Nowadays, I like to remind myself that if a film franchise can take over 20 years and ten movies to figure out its identity (bro-y cop drama to race movie to heist movie to superhero movie), then so can I.

I started this journey on a whim, expecting little, and ended up stumbling into something far exceeding the sum of its parts. I found the genuine love at the core of these movies. That thrill of discovery, and the warmth of finding a home there—why wouldn't you want to invite others into it, saving a seat for them at that backyard barbeque?

Whether others choose to ride with me is up to them, but I've grown enough to know that joy shared is joy compounded. And every time I've shared these movies with someone, it's created a ripple effect of pure delight that I'll gladly work to keep going.

So, with the love of Family in my heart, I, a disciple of Toretto, spread the word of this goofy-ass franchise every chance I get, growing the flock a quarter-mile at a time.

Fast and Furious
BINGO

Han is eating snacks	Michelle Rodriguez choke me please	Impossible technology	someone dies and comes back to life	Corona baby!
Family! Familia!!!	Vin Diesel has superpowers maybe??	homoerotic tension	Car accident but everyone is fine	Fun montage
iconic theme song	LUDA!!!	Free space: Hit the NOS!	Paul Walker is a bad actor (we love him tho)	hand to hand combat
car accident and everyone is not fine	cargo shorts	country where there's no extradition	a really big jump with no broken bones	semi-truck shenanigans
sexy flagger	a problematic comment	"it's been a longgg time/ without you my friend"	The Rock is sweaty	villain turned friend or friend turned villain

By Jules Twitchell

Forgive Me Father, for I Have Drifted: Fatherhood, Daddyhood, and Han Seoul-Oh

Mitchell Xiao Xiao Li

Toyko Drift is arguably the most entertaining Fast & Furious movie: the main character is repeatedly the butt of the joke because he's a white guy named Sean who doesn't speak any Japanese; mid-aughts Tokyo fashion and technology is featured in all of its clunky, grainy glory; and Bow Wow is in it for no reason beyond just having a blast. *Tokyo Drift* is quintessential Fast & Furious with its focus on uniting a rag-tag team of misfits through cars and schemes, but there's one thing that sets it apart from the rest of the Fast movies: Han Seoul-Oh.

Han is introduced in *Tokyo Drift* with no real backstory and dies in an explosive crash about halfway through, but his unflappable charm and constant snacking made him so beloved that the franchise had to loop back and resurrect him in *F9*. Since every Fast movie needs a paternal figure to lead the family, Han is the *Tokyo Drift* version of Dom Toretto—but he offers us a looser, more playful take on this role than Dom does. Han does all the things a father figure must, but he shows us that a father can also be a Daddy by letting go and drifting.

First and foremost, Han Seoul-Oh is the father of this movie: He has a sick garage and a bunch of cars and he works his relationships with his crew to bring the family together. Yes, the premise for the entire plot is that our bumbling protagonist Sean has to move to Tokyo to live with his actual genetic dad, but that guy is basically useless until Han dies. Han is the person who actually teaches our main character what he needs to know to survive, and when he dies, he gives everyone something to fight for, which ultimately turns the crew into a family. Textbook father.

What's more interesting is that Han is also a Daddy in this movie. It's reinforced time and time again that this guy *fucks*—and not only does he fuck, but he's got so many babes that he's comfortable and confident saying no when he doesn't want to (a very sexy quality). Plus, he probably offers his companions an excellent selection of snacks afterwards. This is a stark contrast to Sean, a doofus who doesn't know what to do with himself around women, despite needing to establish that he definitely likes them in the capital-s Straight way. Other characters like DK (the nemesis) and Seans's actual father also canonically have heterosexual intercourse, but Han's interactions with women are different—the others use women to show who they want to be, but Han seems to actually have fun with the women he pursues, rather than chasing them as trophies. He's confident enough in himself to sit back and enjoy the ride, effortlessly embodying this crucial element of the Daddy.

Speaking of riding and paternal roles, Han is the only one who can teach Sean how to drift. Anyone can drive fast, but drifting is about being fully and completely in the moment: One must hit the brakes at the right time, feel the momentum, and surrender to the car. (Hypothetically, of course. I don't know how to drive). When Han drifts, he lets his desires lead—much like how they fuck, all the other characters drift because they have something to prove, but Han just does it for the fun of it. He teaches Sean how to let his guard down and go with the flow, which a strict father can't do—but a Daddy is happy to teach this lesson.

Ultimately, Han shows us that masculinity doesn't have to be so rigid all the time. He relaxes into both the father and Daddy archetypes in the complete opposite way from Dominic Toretto, who can't stop being a father long enough to embrace his inner Daddy. Han, however, fulfils his paternal duty by casually reminding us of the value in truly knowing ourselves and what we want. When things get hard, a father guides by telling us what to do. It takes a Daddy to patiently show us that it's okay to get a little silly, to experiment with our desires, and to reassure us that we'll be ready to act on them when the time is right.

Someone Fast Knocks at the Door
Quinn King

It is the Diesel man. He growls at the explosions. He chews up counterfeit DVDs at the barbecue. Everybody is there. Surprise! It is a race. A car shows up and it is the bad guy kind. The car is fast but not fast enough for the power of family and franchises. This race is for all the nitrous. There is always another race but it is time to go undercover now. Sharp corners and linear time are of no consequence. Drift back to the same scene again and again to see something new: the driver is dead, but maybe they will be alive later, who knows? Mr. Nobody is here and this is a normal name for a normal person. There are piles and piles of favors, a debt for every occasion. You can trade a car for a shinier car for one last job for a pardon. Drive a car fast enough and break physics. Drive it faster and become god. Avenge your dead lover and steal whatever you want. It's a cinematic universe of your own making. Everyone is watching. Your long-lost friend is also your estranged brother and your enemy and your boss and a double agent. Sequel time: something something computers. The cyber hacker nuclear drug lord knocks on the door. The Diesel man will save us, all praise the Diesel man. His bald blood runs on motor oil and acts of service. It is now time to count to 10 in chronological order, here we go: 1, 2, 4, 5, 6, Tokyo, 7, 8, Hobbs, 9, 10. Soon, everyone turns into a flashback and flies away. The Diesel man growls again and swallows the world. Everything is a brief darkness before the next scene starts.

The Great Toretto: A recently discovered original draft of *The Great Gatsby*
T.H. Ponders

In my younger and more vulnerable years my father gave me some advice that I've been turning over in my mind ever since.

"Whenever you feel like street racing anyone," he told me, "just remember that all the people in this world haven't had the same engine work that you've had."

It's the only thing I can remember of my father, and an oddly specific metaphor, but it never left me. Those words crashed against my newly appointed duty, the constructed imperative of justice, and my role in enforcing it, when I joined the LAPD last autumn. I felt that I wanted the world to be uniform and at a sort of moral attention.

But perhaps it was the words of my father that first altered my course, that consumed my instincts, that drove me to assure Agent Bilkins that it wasn't him — Dominic Toretto, who once represented everything for which I had an unaffected scorn. If personality is an unbroken series of stern, silent glares, then there was something gorgeous about him, some heightened sensitivity to the promises of the street racer's life.

It was his extraordinary gift for people, for orphans and strays, a familial readiness such as I have never found in any other person and which it is not likely I shall ever find again. No — Toretto turned out alright at the end; it is what preyed on Toretto, what foul ghosts with lights of blue and red matched his speed in the midnight lamp-lit LA strip of his dreams, that forever ceased my interest in the barbaric trappings and inhuman nature of policing, whose "blind justice" is the result of eyes closed, not covered.

I'll never forget that morning late in July, when my faith in Toretto was most tested, and most shaken. We had just put the first piece of the engine block for the '94 Toyota Supra, the "ten-second" car I owed Toretto, when he stopped and stared at me with a look that surrendered nothing.

"You got big plans tonight, old sport?"

I knew to choose my next words carefully. "Just going out to dinner."

He glanced across the room at Mia and back at me. "You break her heart, I'll break your neck."

"That isn't going to happen." That wasn't just a line, wasn't just my cover. It was true.

He handed me the grease towel, and with his characteristic cool and control said, "I want to show you something."

With fenders spread like wings we scattered light off Toretto's 93 Mazda RX-7, darting between the cars on the streets of LA, until we reached his house. We pulled into the driveway and Toretto motioned towards the garage.

He slid the barn style door to the side, revealing a car the likes of which I'd never seen before. A 1970 Dodge Charger, jet black, demanding a mix of fear and awe by its sleek body and its angular windows— its hood ornamented by a supercharged blower that shone like a dozen suns.

"It's pretty, isn't it, old sport?" He stepped aside to give me a better view. "Know what she ran in Palmdale?"

He paused for added emphasis, as if waiting for me to offer a number he could best without hesitation.

"9 seconds flat. My father was the one driving. So much torque he could barely keep her on the track."

"So what's your best time?"

"I've never driven her." He paused again. "To tell you the truth, old sport, she scares the shit out of me."

He stared at the hood of the car, a fleeting moment of fear in his eyes, as if he was at once determined and afraid of what he felt compelled to say next.

"Look here," he broke out surprisingly. "What's your opinion of me, anyhow?" A little overwhelmed, I began the generalized evasions which that question deserves.

"Well, I'm going to tell you something about my life," he interrupted. "I don't want you to get a wrong idea about me from all these stories you might hear from others."

"I'll tell you God's truth. I am the son of a racer — dead now. I was brought up on the track, because all my family have been racers for many years; a family tradition."

"That there" he said, pointing to a yellowed photograph pinned to the garage wall, "is my father. He was coming up in the pro stock-car circuit. Last race of the season. A guy named Kenny Linder came up from inside, in the final turn. He clipped his bumper and put him into the wall at 120. I watched my dad burn to death. I remembered hearing him scream. But the people that were there said he had died before the tanks blew. They said it was me who was screaming."

"I saw Linder about a week later. I had a wrench, and I hit him. And I didn't intend to keep hitting him, but when I finished, I couldn't lift my arm. He's a janitor at a high school now. He has to take the bus to work every day. And they banned me from the tracks for life."

He looked at me sideways, and I knew why Sargent Tanner believed he was the one responsible. He hurried the phrase "didn't intend" or swallowed it, or choked on it, as though it had bothered him before. And with this doubt, his whole statement fell to pieces, and I wondered if there wasn't something a little sinister about him, after all.

"I live my life a quarter-mile at a time. Nothing else matters. Not the mortgage, not the store — for those ten seconds or less... I'm free."

"I want you on my team, Brian," he said, pocketing the keys to the Charger with reverence, "so I thought you ought to know something about me. I didn't want you to think I was just some nobody without a heart. You see, I don't have friends. I have family."

He wouldn't say another word. His correctness grew in the silence as we drove back to the body-shop and the Supra and the team.

But I was flung once again into doubt by a passing comment from Mia later that day.

"He's like gravity. Everything just gets pulled to him. Even you."

"No," I replied, "the only thing that pulled me in was you."

"Well," she said with her inimitable charm. "It's nice to come first every once in a while."

Though the day felt full of moments of assurance, the doubts of night joined in an unholy choir with this comment and drove me to question everything. Was Agent Bilkins right? Was Mia? Had I just been pulled in by a gravity so strong that I let emotion blind me to my duty?

Amidst the anguish of these memories racing through my mind, I came to the only conclusion that would give me any sort of rest. Reserving judgment was, would have to be, a matter of infinite hope — for my sake, for Mia's sake, for Dom's.

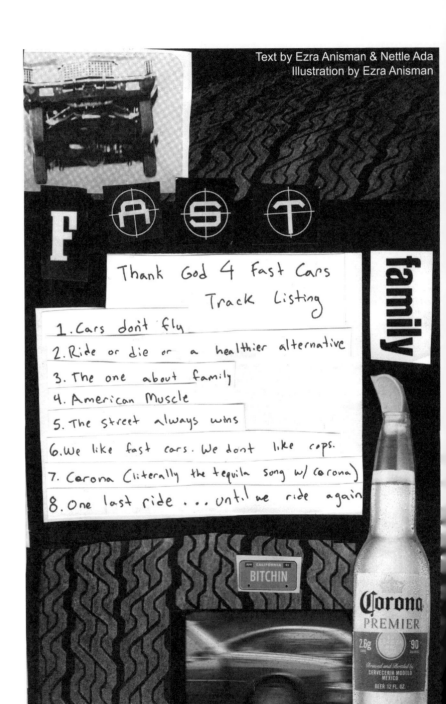

Text by Ezra Anisman & Nettle Ada
Illustration by Ezra Anisman

F A S T

family

Thank God 4 Fast Cars
Track Listing

1. Cars don't fly
2. Ride or die or a healthier alternative
3. The one about family
4. American Muscle
5. The street always wins
6. We like fast cars. We don't like cops.
7. Corona (literally the tequila song w/ Corona)
8. One last ride ... until we ride again

CALIFORNIA
BITCHIN

Corona
PREMIER
2.6g 90
Brewed and Bottled by
CERVECERIA MODELO
MEXICO
BEER 12 FL. OZ.

F69: A View From the Dashboard
Keely Shannon

Dom Toretto hung up the phone and glanced back into the garage. His 1993 Honda Civic EJ1 was wrecked, which was a major setback. And none of the team's cars were ready for the race next week – they all sat in various states of disrepair in the workshop, some with a few scratches and dents from previous races but most waiting for Jesse to fix up an engine or put in new NOS tanks. It was a mess in the garage, and it felt like his life was a mess too. A few hard days' work would get the cars back into shape, he assured himself. It fucking had to. As for his life. . . He pulled the garage door down and slammed it shut, the sound echoing in his wake.

"Civie, that you?" a voice asked once the garage was quiet again, though the space would look empty of life to most humans.

Honda Civic shuddered to life, its engine struggling to start, and began turning around. An orchestra of screeches filled the shop with Civie's slow manoeuvring. When it was finally finished, it could see 1997 Nissan 240SX, 1995 Volkswagen Jetta and 1993 Mazda RX-7 sitting between car lifts and tables covered in tools. They all looked a bit banged up, but nowhere near as bad as itself.

"Yeah, it's me," it said. "You don't have to rub it in, I know I look like shit."

"A flaming pile of shit, maybe," Jett said. "Is there any part of you that isn't burned up?"

"Shut up," Civie said, not feeling up to a smarter response.

"Hey, Jett, we've all been there," Niss cut in. "Cut Civie some slack."

Jett mumbled something Civie couldn't hear but backed off. Civie sighed. "Sometimes I wish this wasn't our life."

"Why?" RX-7 asked from the corner. It was looking in the best shape of all of them; Dom was working on it night and day at the moment. "We've got everything we need here. We're part of a family here."

"Because every other week one of us comes in here looking like this!" Civie burst out. "It doesn't feel like we're part of their family when they're so eager to wreck us. I want. . . I don't know. It would be so much easier if we were like those cars from *Cars*."

"Or like *Transformers*!" Jet said.

"Yeah," Civie said. "They knew what they were doing."

"I'd kill to be able to turn into a space robot. Or even to have weird flexible tyres like in Cars. What good's a sentient car that can't do shit for itself?"

"When are you both getting the chance to watch movies?" Niss asked. "Aren't you locked up in here most of the time?"

"Jesse sometimes watches movies while working," Jett said. "I can't always see the screen, but he plays them out loud."

"When no one else is in the shop, Dom watches car movies while sitting in my back seats," Civie said. "He cries at all of them."

"Has he seen *Dude Where's My Car*?"

"Yeah, he has. I told you: every single one."

"God, you're so lucky," Niss said. "Letty just has the radio on when she's in the garage."

"Yeah, but RX-7 is the luckiest of us," Jett said. "I'd kill to hear all the gossip it does. You'd better hope Dom doesn't work out texting or you won't have all those long calls to listen into."

RX-7 just grunted.

"What's got you in a mood?" Jett said.

"I told it about something I saw the other day," Niss said slowly. "RX-7 thinks it means we'll have to split up."

Jett's engine immediately started in its excitement, clearly not registering Niss's hesitancy. "Whatisitwhatisitwhatisit?"

"I'll tell you both," Niss said. "Just don't say anything about it to the others yet."

"If I do, you can kill me," Jett said.

"Good one," Niss said, "but you know we haven't found a way to die yet."

"Well whatever Dom did that brought us to life in the first place must be reversible. You know I've been trying to see all the stuff on Jesse's computer for months."

"Niss!" Civie interrupted. "Just give us the gossip!"

Niss scoffed. "Okay, so I was at Dom's, and Letty parked me next to Dodge – it says hi by the way – and we were just chatting and then I hear some voices. We shut up just as Dom opens the door and I'm expecting Letty to be behind him, but she wasn't; it was *Brian*." Niss paused, and Civie saw Jett rocking back and forth on its wheels now, engine revving. "Dom and Brian are talking about some upcoming races, looking at us like usual and *then* Brian brings up some argument they had – and they're right in front of my hood now, so I can see it all – and they stare at each other for so long and then *Brian kisses Dom*."

"No," Jett breathed. It, like Civie, had frozen, rapt.

Niss carried on, unable to slow down its story. "They don't say anything, just stare at each other all intense and Brian pushes Dom onto my hood – which is how I got this dent by the way – and they make out on top of me for like five minutes! Then it gets even worse and they stumble into Dodge and . . . well, there were a lot of noises."

Jett had gone shockingly silent, but something clicked for Civie. "So that's why they kissed in me the other day!" it exclaimed. "I was so confused – I thought it was just them being friendly. Wait, am I getting it right that human friends don't have sex?"

It was hard to work out human customs sometimes, especially being locked in garages all day.

"Civie, why didn't you mention that!" said Niss. "And I think so? Dom's never had sex with friends. He only has sex with Letty. Or he used to."

"What does that mean?" Jett whispered. "What happens if she finds out?"

"We'll get broken up," RX-7 said from its corner. "Humans hate it when other humans lie to them about sex."

"They do?" Niss asked.

"Watch a goddamn movie, Niss!" Jett exclaimed.

This was some gossip alright; it could change everything, and probably not for the better.

"We've got to bring this to the rest of the cars," Civie said. "When's the next big race?"

"Next week," RX-7 said. "I heard Dom on the phone earlier – everyone will be there. Good time for a council meeting."

"Excellent. We'll have a vote there about what to do. I do not need more work right now, but we've influenced bigger stuff in the past, haven't we?"

"We've got to be careful, but Dom's easy to influence. Drive slow for him twice in a row when he's just been with Letty and he'll start thinking about breaking up with her."

"Okay, good," Civie said, feeling a lot better despite its still-steaming body. None of this improved its current situation, but it was nice to remember that they all weren't as helpless as they sometimes felt.

"Now turn the music up, Jett."

Factory Issued: *The Fast and the Furious* and the Toyota Supra Mark IV as Transition Narrative
Max Turner

In a franchise where cars represent everything from sex to parenthood, it seems natural to consider how they might also represent the characters' relationships to gender. *The Fast and the Furious* (2001), in addition to its laughable editing, casual racism, and rampant homoeroticism, gives us a prime example of 'car as gender' in the form of Brian O'Conner's Toyota Supra Mark IV. In the context of some trans people's reference to their preoperative bodies as 'factory issued,' it is possible to read Brian's relationship to the Supra and its rebuild as analogous to the trans experience of creating a body that we choose for ourselves through the process of transition.

Brian starts the movie driving the iconic bright green Mitsubishi Eclipse 2G GS, and it becomes immediately clear to the audience that he's uncomfortable in this car; he struggles to control it and makes frequent mistakes. In the initial street race against Dom, the car is literally falling apart around him as he drives. We also learn from interactions with Brian's superior officer, Tanner, that the Eclipse was a loaner from the impound lot and was already modified when it was given to them. To Brian, the Eclipse was 'factory issued' in that he didn't build it, he doesn't know how to handle it properly, and that makes him nervous. The film presents an early contrast to this tension with Dom's Mazda RX7, the interior of which is "handmade with an experimental feel" and which he drives with perfect, collected confidence.[1] While some of the difference in their comfort levels can be chalked up to experience, it's clear that Brian's loss in that race also comes from his disconnect from the Eclipse. As Dom points out, Brian "never had his car." In spite of his natural talent and enthusiasm, Brian literally cannot win in this 'factory issued' vehicle, which is a painfully familiar feeling to many trans people trying to live their happiest and most successful lives without access to gender affirming care.

The rebuild of the Toyota Supra Mark IV around the midpoint of the movie marks a transformation for Brian, both literally and allegorically. For the first time, Brian has a hand in building his own vehicle, and the difference that this process makes in his confidence becomes apparent by the end of the film. In direct contrast to his earlier race against Dom in the Eclipse, Brian driving the Supra in the final drag to beat the train "finally finds that special zone [...] his face reflects a serenity we haven't seen before. [...] The car is speaking to him as none have before."[2] At this moment, Brian is experiencing the euphoria of the first beach day bare-chested or the first correct gendering by a stranger — the feeling of moving through the world in a form that you know intimately and choose for yourself.

The collective nature of the Supra's rebuild is also central to Brian's allegorical transition. As isolating and lonely as the early days of transition may feel, the reality is that nothing happens in a vacuum, particularly not gender. How many trans people have, on purpose or entirely by accident, adopted the mannerisms, personal style, and even the names of the people around us as part of our

[1] Gary Scott Thompson, *The Fast and the Furious*, directed by Rob Cohen (2001; United States: Universal Pictures), transcript, 24.
[2] Thompson, 98.

transition? Our gender identities are always influenced by our social circles and society at large because gender is fundamentally a social construct. The same is true for Brian's Supra: Jesse chooses the shocks, Vince welds in the roll cage, Leon puts in the brakes, Dom installs the engine, and Mia decorates the body. The car, as gender, is a group project. In a franchise whose overarching theme is the importance of family, the involvement of Brian's found family in the construction of his car and identity seems not only appropriate but necessary; the unspoken truth of the Supra's rebuild in the movie is that Brian *could not* have done it alone. It took the expertise, time, and love of the rest of the crew to help Brian reach that moment of serenity in the Supra, just as every one of us is supported along our gender journey by the people with whom we choose to share it.

In the end, the rebuilt Supra doesn't win Brian the race against Dom and the train. You could even say that the 'car as gender' allegory falls apart at the end of the movie, when Brian hands Dom the keys to make his getaway from the cops and stays to face the consequences. On the other hand, we can see Brian's sacrifice as representing the solidarity that we show one another as trans people, the permission we give to others to be themselves by openly and proudly being who we are, even in the face of oppression and punishment by authorities. Brian starts the movie with a career in law enforcement because his dad was a cop, driving a car that he was given by his employer, but his growth as a character has him stepping away from the parts of his life that were chosen for him in favour of the things and people that he chooses for himself. The final moments of the film show Brian giving Dom the very literal gift of freedom in the form of the Supra — from the cops, from the past, and from the 'factory issued' life that Brian himself has escaped with Dom's help. It may not look like the keys to a car, but trans people give each other and ourselves this gift every day.

Earthrise on Tej and Roman
Max Ramirez

Have you ever cried watching the earth rise on the helmets of Tyrese Gibson and Chris "Ludacris" Bridges?

I have.

Sitting in the theater in June 2021 — for the first time since the *CATS* (2019) rowdy screening at the Alamo Drafthouse in February 2020 — KN95 on tight, I wonder if people or movie theaters have always smelled this bad. I watch Roman and Tej successfully exit the atmosphere in a Ford Pinto souped up by Sean, Twinkie, and Earl from Tokyo Drift, who have in the intervening years become spacecraft engineers or something. Who cares why?

I tear up, unexpectedly. I think about how scared I am of space, and how scared they are of space. I've changed so much since I last saw a movie at the Century 20 Daly City, and they've changed so much since *2 Fast 2 Furious* (2003). I imagine doing something existentially terrifying with someone I've known, chosen to work with, to be family with, for twenty years. I think of Robert Morse as Bert Cooper, in the mid-season finale of season 7 of *Mad Men*, sitting on his couch watching the moon landing.

"Bravo."

Stunt Intimacy

Lillie E. Franks

"The motor vehicle action sequences depicted in this film are dangerous. All stunts were performed in controlled environments with professionally trained stunt crews on closed roads. No attempt should be made to duplicate any action, driving or car play scenes portrayed herein."

Every movie in the Fast & Furious series starts with that warning. It's an elegant safety solution, because if there's one thing people who imitate car stunts love, it's following written directions.

But what this disclaimer *really* does is set the attitude of the audience towards the action. We are spectators. While of course we relate to the characters on screen, we are also impressed by them. These are not everymen to imagine ourselves as. They are Sherlock, not Watson; they're the Doctor, not the companion.

Expertise is central to Fast & Furious. The main characters are the ones you call when you need someone to make a car go very fast and then do something it shouldn't do. That's the fun of the movies; it's exciting to watch people who are experts at something do that thing under stressful circumstances.

But they're also experts in something else: relationships. There's a striking similarity between the way that Dominic Toretto's crew approaches cars and the way they approach each other. For every scene of them driving a car perfectly despite adverse conditions, there is one of them doing the same thing for relationships. This is the other half of the series' appeal. Cars battling other forms of transportation is great fun, but it's the love the characters have for each other that makes their world feel like home.

You might not expect these forms of expertise to go together. In many movies, characters who live at the border between unrealistically talented and straightforwardly superhuman are cold and aggressive. These characters are warm and gentle, and their philosophy of family doesn't ask you to earn anything. Their driving makes them an elite, but their kindness makes them approachable.

Except, it's a little more complicated than that. Because the crew's expertise in intimacy in Fast & Furious has a showy quality, much like their driving. This isn't the fumbling intimacy of a family night around the fire. This is full throttle intimacy, down a mountain road with nitro boosters. Dom Toretto loves his family at 80 miles per hour with bullets flying; he loves them when they lose their memory, when they work with international criminals against him, and when a cyberterrorist uses that love to make him her pawn.

These characters do emotional stunts, of a sort. They may not exactly be jumping cars off of trains, but they do engage in behavior that's risky for relationships. They make fun of each other, even at what could be sensitive moments. They push on each other's insecurities. They leave important things in silence, sometimes for years. They go for long periods without talking to each other and reappear suddenly asking for big favors.

But none of this feels unsafe, because it's carried off with the careless nonchalance of experts. Just like Dom Toretto's unflappable cool and low, gravely voice turn a car drifting under a truck from something terrifying to something cool, the crew's manner makes their relationships look safe just when they should look stressed. The characters are always certain of themselves, and certain of the reaction they'll get from others. They rarely need reassurance and, with the exception of a few comedic bits, they never come off as awkward or stumbling.

I love this world. But at the same time, I have to call that what it is: fantasy. These are professionally trained stunt crews on closed roads. The script is the controlled environment that makes them possible. We know these characters will be alright because we know how good they are at caring for each other, at being willing to do anything and everything for family. But you can't drive like the characters in Fast & Furious, and I don't think you can build relationships like them either.

The crew handles relationships the same way that they handle cars. And as much as I love that simile, there comes a place where it breaks down. If you set yourself to it, you could become every bit as good and confident with cars as... well, maybe not as the characters, but as the performers who portray them. A car is consistent and obedient. Becoming a master of it is simply a matter of practice and time.

The same is not true of relationships, at least, not in the same way. Driving one car is basically similar to driving another car. The same is wondrously, fantastically untrue of people. Knowing one person is not the same as knowing every person — in fact, it's not even the same as knowing that same person a year ahead or ago. And that means that you can never have the same unshakeable confidence in relationships as you can with driving. You can't always look cool, even around your family.

That doesn't mean you can't be good at relationships. On the contrary, you very much can. But being good at relationships doesn't look like being good at stunt driving. It doesn't look like effortless poise and smooth, clean movements that hide your expertise under their simplicity. It looks like accepting awkwardness. It looks like being willing to be too enthusiastic or too weird. Being good at relationships doesn't mean you won't be awkward; it means you've learned how to roll with it, and pull the other person along with you. Relationships are above all sincere, and sincerity resists polish.

I like to imagine an awkward Fast & Furious: Dom Toretto unsure if Letty wants suggestions or sympathy. Tej wondering if a joke will bother Roman or not. Hobbs and Shaw checking in with each other during their banter. A movie about people constructing a family, not just relying on it. I don't think it would necessarily be a better movie series, but it would be a more accurate one. And in a way, I think it could bring the warmth that I love in Fast & Furious even closer to its audience.

Fast & Furious is about cars that are fast, and also furious. But all of them are driven by humans who have built connections with each other. Those connections can be shaky. They can be awkward and even painful. But that doesn't stop them from also being family.

The Real Fast Is the Furious
We Made Along the Way
Rebecca Kling

Contributor's note: This is an acrostic. I'm so very sorry.

The two trans women faced off, their argument filling the room. Jessica continued to insist that it was the greatest movie franchise to ever grace the silver screen, while Cathee claimed it had one idea that it drove ("DROVE," she screamed) into the ground.

Helping no one were the empty beer bottles and smoked joints that littered the apartment. Someone had put on *F9*, which had been the perfect platform for Cathee to start her critiques.

"Even if there had been enough oxygen," Cathee shouted at Jessica, "It's supposed to be a series about driving! A series about—"

"Family!" interrupted Jessica. "A series about family!"

Across the room, the rest of the friend group sat on the couch, their heads swiveling back and forth like they were the audience at a tennis match. A stupid, drunken, stoned, tennis match between two BFFs who nevertheless seemed ready to strangle each other.

Sam tried to be a mediator, as they often did, inserting, "If nothing else, I think we can all agree the movies are fun, right?"

The question sent Cathee pacing across the room, muttering to herself. "Fun? We're so past fun. Racing a tank. Racing a helicopter. Racing a submarine, even. But space? What kind of Fast-ian bargain would allow such absurdity?" Cathee looked up to see if anyone had noticed her clever pun, but no one acknowledged the wordplay.

Aiden got up from the couch to refill his empty cup with whiskey and snag a slice of now-cold pizza. The living room was pleasantly crowded with folks over for Jessica's birthday. For better or worse, this seemed to give Jessica the home-field advantage.

"Now, maybe Sam has a point about fun, Cathee," Jessica continued, "Fun. Family. Friendship. Fast cars. Furious...ly repressed homosexuality." A few laughs from the friends on the couch. Jessica paused, gesturing with a drink in her hand as if that would bring the next thought to mind.

"Don't!" Cathee pointed a finger at Jessica and slowly paced towards her. "Don't you dare use alliteration with me!" Her voice fell to a whisper. "You know my father was killed in an alliteration accident. My dad, dead. My papa, perished." She traced a line down her cheek indicating the path of a single tear.

The room, now silent, turned to Jessica to see how she would respond.

"Have you considered," Jessica began, "the deeper question? The question of what The Fast Saga (as it's known to us Fastianatos) has to teach us about each other?"

"Each other?" Cathee's energy seemed to be waning, as if she was being drawn in by the growing spark in Jessica's eye.

"For what if we, the friends in this very room, are the Dominic Torettos and the Paul Walkers of our lives?" Jessica looked each friend in the eye as she asked her question.

"Um," piped in Sam, from the couch, "I think the character's name was Brian O'Conner. The actor was Paul Walker."

"Right!" Jessica seemed triumphant, as if Sam had somehow proven her point. "We are the Paul Walkers and the Mia Torettos and whats-her-name, Gal Gadot's character who-"

"It's Gisele," said Sam. "Gal Gadot's character's name was Gisele. She fell to her death, I think?"

"Our very own Gisele," Jessica seamlessly interjected. "The Fast Saga teaches us that, no matter how ridiculous our circumstances, we can come together to pump in the nitrous oxide, give ourselves a boost, and speed our way to victory. When we focus on family, no red light can stop us. When the chips are down, and the odds are out, and the ref is ready to call the whole game, that's when we need films like *Fast X*, only in theaters May 19, 2023." Jessica concluded, looking very pleased with herself, and bowed to no one.

"Utterly ridiculous," said Cathee, plopping down into an empty chair.

"So, should we watch another one?"

*Artist statement on pg 146

On the Importance of Looking
Dizzy

I think everyone wants to be objectified just a little bit. Not dehumanized, stripped of personhood. Not coarsely, not cruelly, but seen as an object of desire, a thing worth having.

I remember hands on me like I was a side of meat the first time I went to a gay bar. Or, the first time I went to a gay bar with the intention of being touched, seen, desired. I was 19, and it was a real bash, a charity benefit. It was a converted warehouse space in the heart of Austin and the walls were hung with distasteful sculpture, gaudy Warhol-esque portraits, and woodblock prints of tied up men, faces contorted in some kind of ecstasy, some kind of agony. On the little patio outside, ivy crawled up brick walls, penned in on three sides. It wasn't my first time sneaking into a venue on false pretenses, but it was my most audacious—a friend and I talked our way past the door without showing ID, with the cover story that we were last-minute replacements for the no-show models on the guest list. My friend ended up on stage midway through the night, posing like he was born for it while artists sketched and sculpted him. I melted into the crowd, tearing off the name tag that labeled me a model as soon as I was through the front door. I was there to be seen, consumed even, but not laid bare on the page quite like that. I avoided the bar; the drinks were free and IDs were being checked at the door, but what if someone asked? The trays going around the room, carried by fit young men in jockstraps, covered in plastic shot glasses shaped like genderless asses and filled with something neon and strong—those felt safe, and I stuffed the glasses in my pockets like a magpie building a nest out of souvenirs. Yellow, orange, red, all the colors of a sunset, all equally candy-colored and whiskey-strong.

On other nights, I had talked my way past doormen or jumped fences to see punk bands at venues that had never heard of "all-ages," or to meet up with near-strangers who didn't know how young I was, or just to get drunk somewhere that wasn't my living room. This party, however, was my first time going somewhere for no reason other than that it was gay, and loud, and full of people. I don't remember how I was dressed, who I spoke to, but I remember the feeling of moving from the gallery to the bathrooms to the dance floor and being watched, assessed, considered. I remember being cornered out on the patio by a man with cigarette-breath, kissing him until the stale air inside was better company. I remember being touched on my shoulders, my waist, my ass, hands made invisible by the dim lights and press of bodies. The feeling of being wanted was stronger than the shots.

When we talk about the male gaze in film, we are often talking about the eye of the camera. Not everyone is familiar with the concept, but everyone understands it intuitively. The camera, usually wielded by men, imposes straight male patterns of desirability on the subjects, usually women. Megan Fox in *Transformers*, walking by the side of the road, the camera's eye that of a bus stop lecher, dragging from her feet to her face, lingering molasses-slow on her hips, her tits. In the theater, the camera becomes the audience, each of us implicated in its gaze becoming ours, its desires becoming ours. What we talk about less, as a society, is the way men look at each other, the way gay men look at each other and themselves. Queer flirtation is substantively different from straight flirtation; with queer sexuality there's a level of risk, a physical threat, inherent in face-to-face interactions with someone whose sexuality is unknown. Straight people are socially permitted to interact with each other flirtatiously in public spaces, and while a straight person approaching a stranger or acquaintance might be seen as uncouth, they will rarely be seen as deviant. A man can approach a woman at a bar, and he might get laughed off, but rarely accused. The same cannot be said for queer people; the risk of engaging in flirtation with a straight homophobe is simply too great, so much flirtation has to take place subtly. Looks and codes develop, ways of communicating covertly that those not receptive to it might not notice.

Robert Yang, queer theorist and game designer, writes in his essay "The Tearoom as a record of risky business" about the difficulty of assessing risk while cruising public restrooms. The visitors to tearooms—as the sorts of public restrooms you find in campsites and rest stops were called in the '60s and '70s—developed complex rituals of stance and eye contact to ensure mutual consent without stating anything explicit; an explicit offer could be punished. There's a difference between someone looking at you and someone cruising you, making eye contact with their zipper already open, looking you up and down. Assessing. Considering.

I started taking hormones in 2017, started wearing my closet-full of dresses out in public on nights other than Halloween. I shaved off my beard, grew my hair out, learned how to blend my eyeshadow and contour my cheekbones. I learned from a girlfriend how to use orange lipstick on my jaw to mask the faint blue tinge of whatever facial hair electrolysis couldn't fully eliminate. The arc of my twenties, a decade that lined up almost perfectly with the 2010s, went from twink, to jock, to femme, to futch, a label I always call a joke made up by lesbians when straight people ask me what it means (but which I secretly adore). I have a complicated relationship to gender, a complicated relationship to the idea of "passing," as though being mistaken for cis is my highest calling, but I can at least look the world in the eyes and say "I am a woman." Most of the time, the world listens. Some of the time, it agrees.

The ways that gay men look at you, watch you, when they want you, can sometimes be crude. Frightening, if you're not accustomed to it. Despite that, being cruised carries a level of subtlety that's always made it feel safer and less threatening to me than when it comes from straight men. Gay men look at me like they're hungry for me a lot less frequently than they used to. When I haven't hidden my beard shadow as well as I like, when my clothes are a little too bulky to see the shape of me, they do, and the looks are still a little flattering, but it's not thrilling, not electric like it used to be. They're missing information. They see a version of myself that hasn't really existed for years, the version of me with an M on her driver's license and a deep well of discomfort kept under lock and key. I always want to walk right up when they're watching me, cruising me, break the thin membrane of plausible deniability and say, "if you knew what you were actually looking at, you'd be a lot less interested." I never do.

For much of film history, rules similar to the covert code of cruising applied to depictions of queerness. Replace the threat of homophobic violence with the threat of critical failure and economic hardship, and the reasons are apparent: directors wanted to show themselves off without falling afoul of the hetero-dominant studio system. Even in recent years, queer sexuality is largely portrayed subtextually. Many people have written about homoeroticism in the Fast & Furious franchise, but the analysis is often sharply lacking—cheap clickbait articles that rarely go further than crude jokes that run like, "See, they're big men, and they have big muscles, and sometimes they hug so, probably they're gay, I think."

If we look a little deeper, there's a deep, rich seam of homoerotic displays; the men of the Fast and the Furious watch each other, they gaze at each other with the same deep, sublime reverence that they look at their cars, their prize positions. My favorite example of this is in the second movie, 2 Fast 2 Furious. Brian O'Conner is attempting to woo Monica Fuentes, who's embedded with a drug lord. O'Conner deploys a maneuver he calls the "stare and drive," driving aggressively with his piercing blue eyes locked on the person in the passenger's seat. His childhood friend, Roman Pierce, notices this and seems upset, saying, "He got that from me."

Are we meant to believe Roman instructed him explicitly in this? Perhaps that Brian sat in the back seat taking notes while watching Roman use it on someone else, some other woman? These explanations strain credulity; the simplest is that Roman did the "stare and drive" with Brian himself. When Brian turns his gaze on a woman, Roman seems hurt, betrayed, as much by this as by their criminal past.

I leapt into the t4t dating pool as soon as I came out, but when my presentation shifted from simulation of a man to approximation of a woman, the eyes on me changed, too. The subtleties and ceremonies of gay cruising gave way to the leering gaze of straight men. My first night out in a dress, I spent the night at a bar I like, watching the intricate mating dances and assessments of queer people under the scrutiny of a straight venue. On the bike ride home, three different men catcalled me. One of the men was polite, the second was aggressive, the third was drunken and incomprehensible. I went from flattered, to afraid, to angry in three-quarters of a mile.

It's not as though I didn't know what I was getting myself into when I transitioned—I'd spent enough time riding home with women or staying up late swapping stranger-danger horror stories to expect catcalling. I wasn't a stranger to it, either. Wolf-whistles, esoteric and explicit pet names, even just a "hey there," loud enough, with the right inflection... hang out in gay bars long enough and you'll hear them all. It is—it was—a thrill, powerful and dangerous, every time. I was prepared for catcalling, and the strange mix of feelings that come attendant. I wasn't expecting to feel affirmed, a kind of bone-deep sense of being seen, and I wasn't prepared for the depth of the fear. I love that creepy dudes see me as a woman, enough to see me as desirable, as an object of desire. As much as I hate to admit it, I love that I pass. I hate the fear.

I wasn't a stranger to fear, either. If you're visibly gay enough to get catcalled by men, you're visibly gay enough to get beer cans thrown at you from the windows of passing cars. One night in my early twenties, I was walking home with a friend—you learn fast not to walk home alone if you can help it—with a twelve-pack of Pearl under my arm, minus the six or seven we'd already drank. We were waiting to cross the street when a black sedan plastered in college sports team stickers stopped at the red light, its tinted windows rolled up. My heart sank when the window rolled down. Someone from inside hollered "faggot" out the window, the opening salvo. I forgot how to shut up, too drunk and young and angry, and yelled back, telling them to fuck off, keep driving. They escalated, throwing a half-empty can at me, close enough to spatter cheap beer on my boots. My aim was better, and my cans were still full.

In the strangely named *Fast & Furious*—the fourth movie, distinguished from the first only by the amputation of an article—Brian O'Conner and Dominic Toretto are reunited, three full movies after their separation. Dom's main drive in the movie is twofold revenge:

at Brian for his past betrayal, and at the drug lord responsible for the death of his long-time girlfriend, Letty. Letty is replaced almost immediately by Gisele, a woman with whom Dom has precisely zero chemistry. He never responds to her flirtation with anything other than amusement. In her essay "It starts with the eyes," critic Jennifer Smith identifies their first scene together as revealing; Gisele asks Dom to describe his perfect woman, and he lists qualifications that fit her not at all: someone with piercing eyes, who isn't afraid to get engine grease under her fingernails. This description fits Letty, maybe, but Smith argues it fits Brian even better. While Gisele makes half-hearted attempts at flirting with Dom, his relationship with Brian is rebuilt. They work together as partners, working through their tension and misunderstandings like bitter exes forced to reconcile by circumstance. They tease each other. They take care of each other. At the climax of the film, Dom is given a perfect moment of catharsis as Letty's death is reenacted, with Brian in her place. Another film might have put Gisele there, giving Dom the chance to save a different woman, but this movie needs it to be Brian. This is the culmination of Dom's forgiveness made manifest, and it's no accident that he finds catharsis in saving Brian, trapped in exactly the same circumstances as the love of his life, elevating his no-longer estranged friend to the same level. These movies are tied up in the love men have for each other. They may not be explicit, but their eyes say more than their lips.

When I started wearing dresses, I started carrying a knife. I started watching for a different kind of threat. When men catcall each other, grab each other's wrists, waists, and asses in the crush of a dance floor, or follow each other into bathrooms, they're on equal footing. Sexual violence exists among gay men, but by and large, the power dynamic is playful, ebbing and flowing. The subtlety of queer courtship puts a soap bubble-thin membrane around leering, staring, grabbing, cruising. Plausible deniability means denial is possible. I'm still afraid of homophobes and transphobes with half-empty beers in their cars, but despite too many close calls with their kind, they never felt like a threat I couldn't handle. Now, I'm afraid of men with desire, desire that twists too easily into cruelty. Simple rejection can be enough to turn a leering stare into a closed fist, to say nothing of the reaction some men have to finding out they're interested in a woman like me.

I haven't learned to sit with the fear just yet, how to protect myself from it. So, I protect myself from the men, instead. I carry my knife strapped to my thigh under the hem of my dress, and I wear my bike's u-lock like a carpenter's hammer tucked in my belt.

This essay was originally published by Hyperreal Film Club.

I'm A Hater, Hear Me Out
Em Solarova

Part I

After more than half a decade of working in a movie theater, I can't stand this franchise. It's chosen family for the cishets and I hate it.

They're perfectly fine silly action movies, alongside many others that I have no real interest in, but years after quitting my movie theater job, I feel personally victimized by the persistent popularity of the Fast & Furious franchise. I'm a hater, hear me out.

The fervor with which cishet guests care about these movies and their movie-going experiences can only be compared to one other event in the life cycle of a movie theater: Christmas. In both cases, every slight inconvenience becomes a huge personal affront: if we are out of their favorite candy, or the line is too long, or the bathroom is messy, or parking is a nightmare, or...

Sometimes, they show up on a Saturday with tickets for Friday and start arguing with the people who are in "their seats" (who have the correct tickets for the show). When this happens, you have to go in and check everyone's tickets—and the other party is of course the one person in the world who still fully turns their phone off for the movies instead of putting it in airplane mode like an intelligent person or leaving it on like an asshole, so this all now takes that much more time, which you have to spend with the Fast & Furious fans and their crucifixion levels of self victimization. Then you have to explain to the people with wrong tickets that those aren't their seats, and try to reseat them while they argue with you that they for sure bought Saturday tickets (which just couldn't be more irrelevant). You finally talk them down and take them back to the front to switch their tickets, only to find out there are no good seats left where all of their party can sit together. The leader of the group pulls you aside to try to explain to you how important it is that they get exactly what they want because—don't you know what time it is?! It is sacred family time! Oh you're here having to deal with this for minimum wage instead of being with your family? That doesn't matter, because what really matters is that they get their way, otherwise corporate will hear about this! It's family time after all!

This is the kind of energy the Fast franchise brings out in the cishets. It's the "family is most important so everyone else better drop everything else right now" energy, with a ton of urgency and zero awareness that that mentality only works if it applies to them and them only. Perhaps I'm being unfair and people were just as bad during *The Force Awakens* and *Endgame*. The difference is that I personally get the appeal there, unlike with the Fast franchise (and Christmas).

I could further justify my disdain for these films by pointing to how bad the car propaganda is for our collective survival. How the fetishization of cars that are ear-splittingly loud for no goddamn reason, and go faster than one can actually go outside a race track simply for bragging rights, is detrimental for our collective sanity (mine especially). I could probably make this fairly compelling. But one of the great freedoms that I'm learning to inhabit fully since I started medically transitioning (and therapy) is that I'm allowed to just feel feelings. I no longer feel like I need to justify everything as capital-T Truth and be capital-R Right. I'm allowed to dislike these perfectly fine silly action movies and stay as far as I possibly can. Or you know, write into a fan zine about my disdain. So here it goes: I'm annoyed by these films and their persistent popularity.

I wish I weren't. I wish I could just ignore these silly action movies and let the people who like them enjoy them, just like I enjoy all the stupid little things that bring me joy.

The Fast franchise is chosen family for cis people. I wish I could see that, take it, and tell them that I love my queer chosen family kind of like they love these characters. I wish I could use this to foster connection, empathy, and understanding. This, after all, is one of cinema's great, powerful strengths. This is what I love about it! This is among the things that drew me in and kept me working in the film industry in many various forms for over a decade.

But I'm just so tired; even years after quitting, my stomach knots and my skin crawls at the thought of these films. I blame capitalism and the levels of exploitation possible when you convince someone to care about their work, to work in a field they love—but that's for another essay. Anyway, I'm not sure I can explain the excesses of our current stage of capitalism better than by pointing out the existence of *ten* of these silly action films about cars going "vroom."

I'm A Hater Imagining A Better Alternative (Part II)

Dom Toretto and co.'s ability to walk away from car crashes is something to behold and I wish I could confer it on others. Indulge me for a second:

EXT. FLOOR OF GRAND CANYON - DAWN

As the first rays of the sun hit the ground, we find an improvised fire pit of smoldering embers. Behind it, propped up on rocks, sits a 1966 teal Ford Thunderbird. The front hood is badly crinkled and the front wheels lay on the ground nearby.

We hear rustling from inside the car and the convertible roof starts to come down as Thelma and Louise, disheveled, a bit bruised, but really okay, stretch out and climb out of the back seat. (The doors are too damaged to open.)

They begin by rekindling the fire and making breakfast, then spend the rest of the day gathering food and supplies, building a little hut to stay in and really leaning into their cottage-core phase like a couple of ....good friends, of course.

As time passes, they work on repairing the car (ignore the lack of readily available auto parts, not to mention electricity, and just imagine the two of them in overalls, with power tools, Louise teaching Thelma to weld). Wind brings in a piece of newspaper that details their escape from the law and Harvey Keitel's character's refusal to stop without proof of their death. They pack up to relocate, leaving the car behind as evidence, destroying all their progress and making a scene of it. But what about the lack of bodies?! What follows is a thrilling tale of Thelma and Louise faking their own death in a game of cat and mouse with Harvey Keitel's character (whose name I'm simply refusing to Google) before running off into the sunset....and maybe an actual cottage.

Look, all I want is for Thelma and Louise to have the ability to survive a car crash like all these guys and I really don't think it's that much to ask.

Once again, this ire needs not be directed at the Fast franchise alone. I could just as easily tell you I want Thelma and Louise to have Indiana Jones's ability to climb out of the abyss of their own demise, collapse on their knees next to Harvey Keitel's character, comfort him a little, and hug it out. They would look at each other, then down the abyss, then at each other again, and realize—they're alive! This means they are still enemies and the chase restarts anew. This would also be fun!

T for Trans Rights
Emmeline Kaiser

The Swift and the Furious
Evan Obedin

There are only a few things I'm obsessed with, two of which are the Fast Franchise and Taylor Swift. So, I just had to put them together! Enjoy this list of Fast & Furious characters as Taylor Swift albums/eras.

Dominic Toretto: **Reputation**
Songs: "Endgame," "King of My Heart," "New Year's Day," "Look What You Made Me Do"

Dom is extremely protective of his family and loyal to a fault. He will do anything he can to care for them, including traveling across the globe to retrieve Han's body for a proper funeral, risking his own son's safety to protect Letty, and regularly putting his life on the line for others. Dom is also immensely impulsive and aggressive. He attacks others when insulted or unhappy, often before any explanation can be given from the offender.

Reputation represented Swift's transition from "America's Sweetheart" to "don't mess with me," as this era was clad with snakes, leather, and a dark and moody color palette. Don't let the hard exterior fool you, however. This is one of Swift's best examples of a pure love album, filled with the promise of new beginnings and a schoolgirl crush she hopes will become the last love of her life. Just like this album, Dom has a rough and hard exterior—but once broken through, he's a big, sweet softy on the inside.

Brian O'Conner: *Fearless*
Songs: "Fearless," "Love Story," "You Belong With Me," "That's The Way I Loved You," "We Were Happy"

Brian is an adrenaline junkie at heart. He takes risks that are often unnecessary, and places himself and his team in jeopardy in exchange for a big payoff. While largely driven by his emotions, Brian is also honest, protective, honorable, and level-headed, a contrast to Dom's impulsivity and aggression. His love for his found family outweighs everything else, as he ultimately returns to Mia and Jack to make good on his promise of being a father to his growing family by parting ways with his old life for good.

Fearless established Swift as a crossover artist, similar to Brian transitioning from cop to criminal. It remains the most awarded country album in history, including giving Swift her first Album of the Year award at the Grammys. Just like Brian, this album is a true classic and fan favorite for a reason.

Mia Toretto: *Lover*
Songs: "Daylight," "Lover"

Mia is a caring mother and sister who fiercely loves her family. When Owen's crew showed up to kidnap her, she gave Jack to Elena and sacrificed herself to ensure Jack and Elena wouldn't be found. She also helps Brian rescue Dom from the prison bus at the beginning of *Fast 5*.

Drastically different from Dom and *Reputation*, Mia as *Lover* is the rainbow after the storm. Butterflies replaced snakes and pastel pinks, purples, and blues superseded the dark, edgy color palette of the past. Much like Mia fading into the background in later movies, this era was cut short by the pandemic. However, this album and character mark a happy pivot away from the petty drama of the past and into a future filled with love and hope.

Letty Ortiz: **RED**
Songs: "Begin Again," "Everything Has Changed," "Come Back... Be Here," "Run"

Letty is a passionate and driven woman. After losing her memory, she still returns to Dom and their family, helping Dom come back to life multiple times. She often risks her own life, even going undercover in Braga's cartel to bring Dom back home. She's outspoken and not afraid to stand up for herself, telling Brian, "Nobody makes me do anything I don't want to".

Despite being a mix of country and pop, *RED* has the most consistent aesthetics of any of Swift's albums. *RED* is filled with vintage aesthetics and a longing for the past. An album categorized by true, painful heartbreak, it's a cult classic for a reason, just like Letty. *RED* ends on a hopeful note with "Begin Again," and even when Letty lost her way and memory, she was able to return to what mattered most: her family and Dom.

Luke Hobbs: **Speak Now**
Songs: "Superman," "Better Than Revenge," "Mean"

Hobbs is practical, resourceful, intelligent, and courageous with a formidable personality. He is prideful and condescending to his opponents, and uses questionable means to obtain information or get revenge. After the death of his crew, Hobbs becomes an untrusting loner who bashes anyone who gets in his way.

Speak Now is a sharp lean into theatricality. While this album is country, it's a more grown-up and glam version of *Fearless*, much like Hobbs is arguably a more grown-up version of Brian. Entirely self-written, this album was a chance for Swift to prove herself.

Roman Pearce: *1989*
Songs: "Welcome To New York," "Style"

Roman often allows his ego to get the better of him, using his humor and theatricality to distract opponents and disarm strangers. He lives for fame and attention, and is often seen with large groups of women.

Inspired by the golden age of 80's pop, this era was ushered in by Swift's glittery crop tops and freshly cut bob, which aided her evolution to pop stardom. This album was the most awarded in pop history, giving Swift her second Album of the Year award at the Grammys. Focused on her image in the media, this era was full of her star-studded squad, rumors, her public perception, and being labeled as a serial dater. Similar to Roman who's always rolling in style, this era celebrates the youth and freedom associated with growing up.

Han Lue/Seoul-Oh: *Taylor Swift*
Songs: "Teardrops On My Guitar," "Tied Together With A Smile," "I'm Only Me When I'm With You"

Han is a calm, quiet observer. While nomadic, he has always craved stability, especially with Giselle, making her death all the more tragic. His demeanor is a sharp contrast to the rest of the crew and makes him an underrated character, just like this album.

This self-titled era was Swift's debut into the world of music, written while she was still in high school. Swift embraced the "simple girl with her guitar" vibe as she began navigating her place in the music industry, similar to Han craving stability and a place in the world after Giselle.

Cipher: **Reputation**
Songs: "Look What You Made Me Do," "This Is Why We Can't Have Nice Things," "I Did Something Bad"

Cipher is an infamously powerful, tenacious, and manipulative woman driven by greed and arrogance. She is pure chaos and has petty villain energy. While this vibe is not reflective of 95% of Swift's discography, Cipher most closely correlates to *Reputation*. These songs are most representative of the anger and pettiness that Swift was experiencing, and the lengths she was willing to go to in order to claim back her narrative. She didn't care about the public's perception of her anymore, and it showed.

Leo and Santos: **Folklore** and **Evermore**

Name a more iconic duo. Enough said.

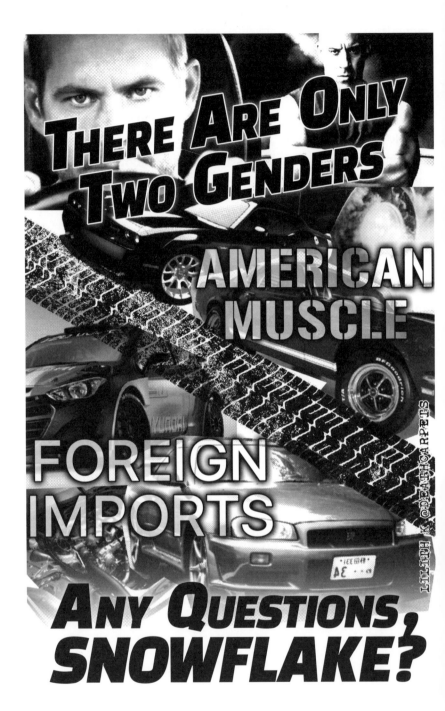

Fast X was released in theaters as we were putting the finishing touches on this book. Once we heard rumors of Dante Reyes' whole deal, we knew we had to sneak him in here somewhere. Many thanks to Lilith for writing this last-minute emergency essay.

Dante Reyes, I Love You
Lilith K.

There was a sticky summer weekend just after I'd started hormones where I was too freaked out by the shit going on in my body and too scared of the looks I got anytime I left my apartment to do anything but watch every Fast & Furious movie in order. Paul Walker had just died, *Furious 7* was on its way, and I needed something to latch onto when my world was so turbulent. It worked and it's just never unstuck.

As deep as my love for the family runs, there's been something missing since *Furious 7*. The obvious answer is Brian O'Connor— Dom just doesn't feel complete without his submissive and breedable ex-cop—but there's more to it. Since then, The Family now seems obsessed with adding to their ranks by turning their villains, shonen-like, into allies. The Shaw brothers, who spent the sixth and seventh movies obsessed with tearing the Toretto clan apart at the seams, were reluctantly turned into allies by the eighth movie. John Cena as Jakob Toretto didn't even get to the end of his introduction in *F9* before his induction back into the family. Cipher, the girlboss hacker with a "maybe she's bisexual, maybe she's just divorced" series of haircuts, managed to maintain her villain status through *F8* and *F9*, but in the opening moments of *Fast X* she shows up, bleeding and affable, at the Toretto house.

At first I was distraught that we had lost another villain, but when she revealed the reason for her surrender to the good guys I was giddy beyond words, screaming at my girlfriend in the theater. Cipher was bested by a new love of my life, Dante Reyes.

Dante's introduction falls in line with F&F's love of an elaborate retcon. He is the son of the crime lord Hernan Reyes from *Fast 5*, now present for the elaborate bank heist in its climax, after which he apparently sat around for four movies waiting for the Shaws and Cipher to get their hits in before hatching his scheme. He often repeats the final words his father said to him: "Never accept death when suffering is owed."

Dante introduces himself to the Torettos by attempting to nuke the Vatican and frame our favorite band of street racing Catholics for it. (Chef's kiss.) He offs his own henchmen and then excitedly details his plans to destroy Dominic to their rotting corpses in a bathrobe and pigtails while painting their nails in lovely pastel shades.[1] Dante then proceeds to run around in silk shirts and snakeskin jackets, giggling like a schoolgirl as his plans for vengeance succeed. He's Heath Ledger's Joker by way of HIM from the Powerpuff Girls in the body of the most terrifyingly built bottom on Grindr.

Dante Reyes isn't avenging the loss of his family: he openly states his disdain for his own father. He is an avatar of queer aggression, singularly obsessed with destroying the Toretto family unit over the theft of his daddy's millions. His presence spits in the face of queer readings of the Fast Family that I have at times held dear, as he

---

1 This was a scene entirely improvised by Jason Momoa. Director Louis Leterrier thought it would be cut from the movie. It divided test audiences, and only made it in at the urging of a British Universal executive, which has a whole host of implications. They wanted to see what Dante was like when he's by himself, when he's not "peacocking" for anyone else. Is this what they think we're like after we go home from hosting drag brunches for impressionable children? Excellent, no notes.

seems to define himself in opposition to their straightness.

(There is a hypothetical scene in the as-yet-unannounced next movie that I can see crystal-clear in my mind: Dominic is strapped to a chair, hopefully naked, while Dante waxes poetically about his life of beauty and finer things outside the gunmetal and khaki confines of Toretto family life. He tempts Dominic with freedom and oral pleasure before Dom is saved by Letty, who runs over Dante with the family Dodge Charger and then announces she's pregnant.)

Years ago, when I first found my way to the franchise in my more Tumblr-brained days, I might have some words to say about how such a gender-nonconforming villain might not be the wisest creative choice in the current global clusterfuck of transantagonism that I don't feel like we need to detail here. But here and now I can only cheer. With two movies left, we've finally got a villain who I not only love, but kinda want to win. I want Dante to destroy this pillar of heterosexual masculinity that my hormonally blitzed psyche latched onto 10 years ago.

Or, at least, maybe in the 11th movie he can show hole.

Zoom Zoom Bish
Emmeline Kaiser

What is Fast If Not Furious Everlasting
Niko Stratis

We got high in the back seat of a run-down Toyota Supra, parked between white lines in a lot below a mall that I no longer remember the name of. We huddled there together, the four of our bodies filling a space meant only for two, passing a joint, listening to Rage Against The Machine and preparing ourselves to be made different by what we were about to witness. As the joint burned away to oblivion, we chased with shots of cheap whiskey to mask the smell of weed on our breath and the dullness on our senses, and stumbled out from our backseat and onto the hard pavement of an Albertan summer day. We pushed each other's bodies with grace and care as we climbed over a folded-forward back seat to exit through the front seat, as we forced ourselves from interior to exterior day and adjusted to the blinding lights of a fluorescent concrete skyline.

Once inside the theater, all of us — once so comfortably huddled tight together – made sure to leave a buffer seat between each other. Prolonged exposure might lead to a prolonged bout of homosexuality, and we were not here for dalliances in the endless fields of queer joy. We were there to become Fast, but to always remain Furious.

The energy in the theater was electric that day, as NOS burned and Axe Body Spray wafted between entrenched heterosexual buffer seats. Men yelled at each car when it roared to life and watched with bated breath as shirts clung to threadbare life on Vin Diesel's bursting chest. We were a little high and a little drunk and a little carried away with living life a quarter-mile at a time, living for all that was possible.

After the movie, when we went to climb back into the car, my hand, guided by exuberant thrills and weed and whiskey, grazed the thigh of a man climbing into the backseat before me. A man tall and gravel-voiced like Vin Diesel himself spun around and shoved me so hard I fell to the concrete, telling me to watch my fag little hands. The other men laughed and planned to go see the movie again the following day, without me there to ruin it for them.

A month later, Nickelback became a sensation, putting the bro back in rock and roll. I told my first-ever girlfriend that I was a transsexual, using language I had learned from the nascent days of internet pornography, as the hit single "How You Remind Me" played on a cheap plastic CD player from Wal-Mart. I was soundly rejected and told that lying about being a little fag was a bad way to break up with someone, which was how I discovered we were breaking up.

The next time there was a Fast and The Furious movie in theaters, I did not go see it—but I did text a girl I was dating using a T9 flip phone to say that I was a transsexual while in line at an Arby's drive-thru. She never replied to me ever again.

I have never seen another Fast and the Furious movie inside of a movie theater, but I am nonetheless ensorcelled by the Fast Cinematic Universe of invincible heroes living only for quarter-miles and family, and have watched every single movie in my own space.

There was a trailer for *Fast X* playing in IMAX at the movie theater when my fiancé and I took each other on a date to see *John Wick 4*. When we first found our seats, the theater was empty. But as the clock ticked closer to the hour of Wick, rows of seats filled with men and women, on dates or in groups, and two men who did not sit with a buffer between them at all.

When the trailer for *Fast X* hit, these two men were alive in their seats, laughing at the absurdity on display as the Toretto family sped fast and furious towards finality. Holding each other in joy, they delighted in Dom dropping out of the ass-end of a jet plane on a highway and racing against time and Jason Mamoa to save his family; they reveled in the reveal of Rita Moreno as the matriarch overlooking all things.

The two men made a loud and solemn promise, right there and then, that they would see this movie together on opening day. There is not enough NOS in the world to keep them apart from this future day spent together. They leaned back in their chairs with deep sighs and fading laughter, spent with all the energy expelled over the course of a two-minute trailer, and said with delighted lilts in their voices, *"Bro, it's a date."* They shook on it and laughed once more.

The energy of aggressively enforced heterosexual energy, which had once pushed me to the concrete of a parking garage in the summer-time in Alberta, has evaporated into the unknown. It is a NOS tank left empty and languishing. I don't even really know what NOS is or does; in all the ten films it has never once been explained, and this is because NOS does not matter. The cars do not matter, nor do the wheels or the pavement or the shirts covering the fine details of Vin Diesel's chest.

The lasting legacy of a franchise about men driving cars so fast — so fast as to burn off all their residual desire to stand close enough to taste each other's sweat — lives in the hearts of all those who have found it, who have loved it and cherished it and held it close. It has lost the toxic bro beating at the heart of it because it was never meant for those bros in the first place. It was for us: curious queers delighting at all of these men as tall as towers, so in love with each other that they would see the world burn, if only so they could drive together one more time. These men, and the women who can punch and drive and roll off rooftops better than goddamn anyone: they are family, and family supports and looks out for each other. Family never pushes someone away because they are scared of what they might represent; they only hold close and tight, clenched in fists and hugs and long piercing stares.

With *Fast X*, our story pulls the curtain and we say goodbye. There is no more to tell in this story; it has given us all that it can. We have come and we have sped and we have been Fast together, but it has been so long since we have been Furious and so let us just be Fast once more, here together at the end. For we have come at last to put Furious things to bed.

Imagining Faster Futures
Contributor Collective

This zine was created in the weeks leading up to the release of *Fast X*, the penultimate installment in the Fast & Furious franchise (allegedly). We asked our friends, contributors, and random trans Twitter users to predict what might happen in the film.

• "I predict they're gonna drive slowly and calmly. I've said this before but this is the one, I just have a feeling." - *Ezra Furman*

• "They're all on VanMoof s3 e-bikes which are a great option that balanced safety speed and reliability well suited for both short city trips and the long distance commute." - *Colin*

• "It turns into like, an educational driving video mid-stunt and they start worrying about traffic laws and discussing safe driving practices, and beyond that, the importance of building a non-car-dependent society, also something explodes?" - *Liz Yerby*

• "Submarine cars, I guess. Car breaks down and is towed underwater by a friendly pack of dolphins." - *Reo Eveleth*

• "Cars must recieve gas through a realistic, fleshy mouth that goes 'yum!' when full. It is never addressed." - *Io*

- "Cipher and Letty kiss. Unclear what happens next, when I think about it my brain turns into hornets and I just start yelling and spinning in circles. My cat had to type this tweet for me." - *Lilith*

- "Letty is going to body swap with the evil lady." - *Anon*

- "I have never seen a single movie from this franchise, but I think all the boy drivers kiss and the girl drivers get together and start a non-profit driving school for underserved youth." - *Maddy C*

- "They'll go faster than the speed of light and time travel." - *Evan*

- "Vin grows hair and, boy, does he grow it long." - *Anon*

- "I've only seen the first movie but if Dwayne or Vin went full Titane with one of their rides that would be pretty sick." - *Alana S*

- "Two words: Robo Brian." - *Mckenzee*

- "Return of zeppelin flight. Cable car chase scenes. Ziplining + NOS. Cars still but rideshare. Evil AI car driven by a hologram of Paul Walker." - *Calvin Kasulke*

- "Tej dies and Roman has an Achilles grieving Patroclus moment, just like full on beating his breast and pounding his chest." - *Dizzy*

- "A Fast & Furious that is just the barbecue at the end. No one is in danger. Just 90 minutes of the family hanging out, drinking beers." - *MJ*

- "It's just a new Chronicles of Riddick movie, this has all been a long con switcheroo." - *Rosemary*

Artist Statements

We asked illustrators featured in this zine to offer statements on their work, if they so desired.

Jillian Fleck: In the year 2023 I set out to create the platonically perfect Fast & Furious film. The true story, the one that the film franchise had been doughnuting around in a destructive gyre, yet has been too cowardly or perhaps too wise to ever fully realize.

The ideal Fast & Furious film is, beyond all things, fast and furious. Before depictions of character, setting, plot, and other such expendable minutia, the ideals of velocity and wrath must be fully realized in all their glory. Circumstantial details are deadweight to the abstract impetus at the centre of this glorious franchise. That force is wailing to be released.

You might be thinking, who am I to undertake such a task? I am but a poor graphic novelist/comic academic/art instructor/orchid enthusiast who must listen to nature sounds to focus and (perhaps worst of all) does not drive. Yet, despite my imperfect nature I am driven in the pursuit of these ideals. Perhaps the myth of Icarus is too, in its way, a Fast & Furious tale.

Marina Crustacean: The Fast & Furious writers would like you to believe that Mia just wants a normal life. If so, explain: drifting expert, designated APC driver, stole a car off a train, beat a bus in a game of chicken, defeated a trained combatant with a frying pan.

J: Worm on a string is a genderless queer icon; it supplants the tough exterior of Dominic Toretto to embody the youthful fun that is the Fast franchise and deliver a big splash of queerness, even in greyscale. (Honestly, I'm just happy to see something weird and queer exist in the world for the sole purpose of amusing another trans person.)

Acknowledgements

Niko & Tuck:

To every writer, illustrator, person with a funny idea and well-wisher: holy moly. You all really came out of every good corner of the universe to bring so many beautiful and fantastic ideas to the table, and we are blessed for your talents. Thank you all who contributed to this zine, directly or indirectly. Sorry to everyone that didn't make it into this one; just know that reading through your work was the highlight of our lives.

Thank you to Casey Plett, Ezra Kupor, Lyn Corelle, Liz Yerby, Kitty McLeod-Martinez, Io, Maddy Court, Yashwina Canter, Shay Mirk, and everyone else who patiently explained how to self-publish and distribute an anthology. Endless additional thanks to Shay for turning a bunch of Google docs into a printable book-shaped item.

Tuck:

First and foremost, all my thanks to Niko Stratis. I still do not understand how you found the time and energy to co-edit (and co-design!) this book, but I am endlessly grateful for it. Thank you for building us increasingly elaborate spreadsheets, fielding my chaotic texts, and generally making this project ten times better.

Thank you to Taegan, Tehya, Seven, MJ, Dayla, and Vivian for watching these silly movies with me. Taegan and Tehya, this thing would never exist without you (for better or worse lol) and I miss you every day.

To every single Gender Reveal patron for generously supporting my work, even when my "work" is "editing a horny haiku about the Rock." To Ozzy Llinas Goodman and Cassius Adair for enabling me to ignore my real jobs and make this instead. To Maggie Cooper for being unreasonably chill when I bailed on a real book deal and launched this pitch call the next day. And to my friends who generously supported me in this project even though most of y'all write real actual books.

To Mckenzee, for everything, forever. To Rhubarb, who just jumped on the keyboard to say "nm-=[[[[[[." (I couldn't agree more.)

And to every trans person making weird queer art despite it all: this one is for you.

Niko:
I would like to thank, before and above all else, Tuck Woodstock, for letting me help on this project even though I was very busy already and a bit of a flake at least some of the time. You really managed to make something special and magical out of an all-trans Fast and the Furious zine, which is no small feat. This is a landmark achievement and I hope you take endless pride in it.

To my fiancé Alysha: Thank you for being patient with me when I was already overworked when I had to stay up late to work on a zine for movies I'm not sure you've ever watched, other than the trailer for *Fast X* we saw at *John Wick 4*. I love you a quarter mile at a time. To all the supporters of my work, and my editors and literary agent who all are endlessly supportive and also never say "why are you working so much on a zine about the Fast and the Furious." Thank you all for getting it.

To the Toretto family: thank you for blessing us with your family, you are beautiful each and every one.

All the love to trans people. I don't know, I had this whole long ass thing about trans people that make art about pop culture but Tuck wrote that already so I'm just gonna say I fucking love trans people and leave it at that.

And finally to you, the reader. Thank you for being here. I love you too.

Contributors

AA & AK: We are a duo of two homosexuals, both alike in dignity (none) and we are in a relationship. AA has never seen the Fast and the Furious (though they did see most of *F9* and were forced to watch the Pontiac in space scene early on in the relationship). AK LOVES the Fast and the Furious franchise but has ADHD and only pays attention to approximately 30% of any film.

Adrian Glenn is a trans man and researcher based in Philadelphia, PA, who likes beans.

aj castle spends an exorbitant amount of time watching films and writing unnecessary film analysis for no one. He is particularly fond of sci-fi horror or any horror that disrupts and challenges hegemonic ideas around gender, bodies, and sexuality. IRL he is a PhD student in women's, gender, and sexuality studies and is somewhat preoccupied with questions around technology and gender, digital media, and the legacy of Mary Shelley's *Frankenstein*.

Al Larned: I'm a non-binary artist from Florida (I know). The work I usually make surrounds my life as a queer person and everything else that comes along with the human experience. Projects like this help me keep my work light and fun; as well as letting me embrace my weird love for the Fast & Furious franchise. As one of the few gays who CAN drive, I'm happy to be here! :)

Alyssa Grimley is a nonbinary writer from Texas who enjoys ghost stories, a nice cup of tea, and watching baking shows with a frankly unnerving fervor. At any given moment, they are probably thinking about birds or WWE lore.

Dakota Hommes is a writer, actor, filmmaker, and game designer. Dakota recently starred in the short film *The Treadmill Switcher*. She used to live in Missouri but now she lives in so-called Seattle. She believes T4T is the most powerful force in the universe.

Dizzy is a poet, essayist, and queer theorist from Austin, Texas. She spends most of her time crying about gender near microphones. In 2019, as part of a joint venture between the Hyperreal Film Club and the Museum of Human Achievement, she was named Expert and Historian of the Fast & Furious franchise. She has a medal to prove it. She can be found at penisweed.com.

Em Solarova is a filmmaker, writer, and cat lad(y). Originally from the Czech Republic, they moved to the USA over a decade ago in search of fame and fortune. Instead they discovered Mexican food and the rest is history. When not searching for the best vegan cheesecake in the 5 boroughs, Em can be found on YouTube as "Person Who," griping about the bio-essentialist, gender binarist nature of their first language: Czech.

Emmeline Kaiser is a mixed gaysian based in Connecticut. They can be found on instagram @emkaisart.

Evan Obedin: I'm an aspiring PA and when I'm not watching Fast or listening to Taylor, I enjoy running my Etsy Shop "2 Craft

2 Furious," spending time outside in nature, and with friends and family.

Ezra Anisman is an artist, a ghoul about town, and all around good time! They live, laugh, love, and work as an audio recording professor in that perpetually moist PNW. Contact them to make an actual Fast & Furious concept album. **Nettle Ada** makes some fun art sometimes.

Gretchen Felker-Martin is a Massachusetts-based horror writer, author of the critically acclaimed novel *Manhunt*, and film critic.

Heather Davidson lives in Glasgow, Scotland. They have hijacked an all-staff meeting to force all their colleagues to listen to their ranking of the Fast & Furious movies not once, but twice. You can find more of their work at heathermade.net.

J is a printmaker, aspiring ex-technologist, and recovering car-person who can be found giving away queer books and zines at TheirOpen.Page. The coolest car they've ever been in is: the Good Burger Mobile.

Jameson Alea is a software engineer and letterpress printmaker in Buffalo, NY. They also host a Fast & Furious fan podcast called Stationary and Sassy. They're only a demolition derby driver in their spare time. Find him online at jamey-alea.com.

Jillian Fleck is a non-binary comic creator, academic, and art instructor based out of Calgary, Alberta. Their graphic novel *Lake Jehovah* was published by Conundrum Press, and their work has recently been included in *Alberta Comics: Home* from Renegade Arts Entertainment. They are very sleepy all the time.

Jules Twitchell is a queer and non-binary Fast & Furious fan. Han is their favorite character. They have a gremlin dog named Mavis, and they like to embroider and watch lots of movies with friends.

KJ: I'm a 24-year-old trans and non-binary person living in Brooklyn, NY. I'm currently in grad school to be a therapist, which I truly love. I love to write, collage, embroider, skateboard, spend time with friends, and watch silly dumb movies for comfort. I love to explore the concepts of grief and transformation in the poetry I write and art I make. Grateful 2 be here on this earth and get to exist alongside so many wonderful people and places and things. <3

Keely Shannon (they/them) is a writer, editor and amateur skateboarder based in Norwich, UK. When they aren't writing car movie fanfiction, they work as deputy editor for *LookDeeper Zine*, a publication run by and for disabled people. Recently, they accidentally watched the fourth Fast & Furious movie thinking it was the first and didn't realise until a few days later.

Kim Kuzuri is non-binary butch queer who has unironically loved Tokyo Drift since being part of its tiny transformative fandom in the mid-aughts. Most recently their writing has appeared in *Best Bondage Erotica of the Year, vol 1* and *Best Women's Erotica of the Year, vol 7*. Before their life was blessed by the birth of the F&F franchise and its many aspirational gender feels, they won some youth poetry awards for works exploring the familial impact of Japanese American incarceration and the Asian diaspora. This poem is their first return to the medium since seeking gender affirming care.

Lee Sessions: When not writing poems about inanimate characters in the Fast and the Furious multiverse, Lee works as a curator, researcher, and union organizer. He lives in Brooklyn with his husband, three cats, and lots of furniture scavenged from the street.

Lilith K is a satanic lesbian transgenderthing who makes podcasts, tabletop RPGs, and a smattering of other internet ephemera. You can find her @deathcarpets anywhere on the internet she wants to be found.

Lillie E. Franks is a trans author and eccentric who lives in Chicago, Illinois with the best cats. You can read her work at places like Always Crashing, Poemeleon, and Drunk Monkeys or follow her on Twitter at @onyxaminedlife. She loves anything that is not the way it should be.

Malachi (they/he) lives in Red Hook, Brooklyn, and refuses to learn to drive. They write a newsletter about cooking, being trans, and having a dead dad (funner than it sounds) at kitchenmaledictions.substack.com.

Marina Crustacean is an estrogen enthusiast and recovering wolf girl with too many hobbies; these include writing, photography, digital art, and the perpetual overthinking of various mass media franchises.

Mattie Lubchansky's debut graphic novel *Boys Weekend* is out now from Pantheon. They think privately owned cars should probably be illegal (la familia excluded).

Max Ramirez (he/they) is a copywriting flunkie/current barista based in San Francisco, California. They once took a Buzzfeed quiz that told them he's a Roman and he's spent a few years coming to terms with that.

Max Turner is a genderqueer transmasc lesbian of Irish descent living on Algonquin land in so-called Ottawa, Canada. They are a devoted listener of Gender Reveal, a longtime Fasthead (???), and an evangelist for the video essay "2 Bi 2 Furious" by Ben from Canada on YouTube. They hope that this zine will convince more people that everyone from the Fast & Furious franchise is trans and gay and should, in fact, kiss. They also plan on subjecting their cats, Princess Peach and Princess Daisy, and their dog, Blueberry Muffin, to a complete rewatch of the franchise, alongside their long-suffering fiancée.

Mckenzee Griffler (she/her) is a filmmaker, Gender Reveal contributor, and Normal Girl who would've strongly suggested maybe not calling it "Race Wars" in the first movie, had she been in the writer's room.

Miche Devey: My pronouns are they/them and I reside in Glasgow, Scotland. Been a fan of the Fast series for a while now, despite the fact that I cannot drive. Nor will I ever learn to. I do, however, use Fast & Furious-branded pomade[1] to style my hair and that keeps me smelling like I'm living my life a quarter mile at a time.

Milo (they/them/their), 29, nonbinary, autistic, is just kind of out here, sometimes draws, always has some niche stuff they're worked up about, and never manages to keep it concise.

Mitchell Xiao Xiao Li is an avid cook and crossword aficionado based in Montreal, where they live with their perfect angel demon cat, Bean Curd. Their ideal day involves pastries, biking for hours at a time, and lounging in a park with good wine and good company. They aspire to one day make a perfect bowl of noodles.

Niko Stratis is a transsexual writer who saw the first Fast and The Furious movie on opening day in a movie theater in Calgary,

---

1 Miche: the pomade is really real and it smells great btw: suavecito.com/collections/sua-vecito-x-fast-and-furious

Alberta the month before trying to come out as trans for the first time. Her work has appeared in outlets like Bitch, Xtra, Catapult, Huffington Post and Autostraddle. She currently writes a newsletter titled Anxiety Shark. She lives in Toronto, Ontario with her fiancé, one dog and two cats. She is a Cancer and a former smoker.

Quinn King is a queer trans poet and her work has appeared in Spillway, Pedestal Magazine, The Binnacle, Black Heart Magazine, SHIFT, Portals, and Quarterlife. She is originally from Seattle but now lives in Calgary, Alberta with her wife, kid, and two rowdy cats. She misses the ocean.

Rebecca Kling is a Chicago-based trans advocate. Find her online at bwcollab.com.

SamuelAnimates (they/them) is a researcher and artist who wants to make public health more human. They love to experiment with different media, and to bring in their love of sci-fi and bright colors into professional spaces.

S. Mirk is a comics journalist, author, and prolific zine-maker. During the course of laying out this zine, they were inspired to draw Cipher bowl cut fanart and had a dream wherein the seventh F&F film was called *Fast & Furious 7: Star Wars*. You can see their art and cute dog on Instagram @mirkdrop.

Skylar Pape is a poet who has somehow embraced the chaotic nickname Skylar "Sweet Cheeks" after a host of her favorite open mic commented that it would make a good stripper name. Skylar's other work can be viewed on their blog at tgirlpoetry.com.

Tehya: I am a professional namer with a keen eye and passion for graphic design. I can help you reveal your inner strengths and assets through the power of art. I am a firm believer that everyone has an inner Fast & Furious name. This masterpiece art will help you to quickly and furiously unlock your name and along with it, your fate.

T.H. Ponders (they/them) is a designer, writer, and multidisciplinary creator from Boston, Massachusetts. Their work includes the queer fairy folk tale The Wanderer, and the narrative art history podcast Accession. They drive a 2010 Toyota Sienna and begrudge the Fast franchise for not having more minivans.

Tuck Woodstock is a journalist, educator, and resident gender detective. Tuck hosts the long-running podcast Gender Reveal, where they've interviewed at least nine of the people on this contributors list. He now lives in New York, where he never has to drive. Find Tuck at tuckwoodstock.com.

THE OFFICIAL D&D CLASSES OF EACH OF THE FAST & FURIOUS CHARACTERS

(TUCK TOLD ME THERE WAS AN
EXTRA PAGE IN THE ZINE, SO..)

DOM → BARBARIAN
BRIAN → HUMAN WARRIOR, SPECIFICALLY
TEJ → ARTIFICER
HOBBS → PALADIN
ROMAN → BARD
HAN → DRUID BUT FOR CARS
LETTY → WARLOCK
RAMSEY → WIZARD
N CIPHER N → ROGUE
SHAW → MONK ??
M'IA → CLERIC
MR. NOBODY → DM

BY CALVIN KASULKE,
WITH SIGNIFICANT COUNSEL
BY TUCK WOODSTOCK

PLEASE DIRECT ALL DISPUTATIONS
AND/OR CHARACTER BUILDS TO
NOSTRADOMEOUS @ GMAIL.COM